Anniversary
A LOVE STORY

Michael Adamse, Ph.D.

Health Communications, Inc.
Deerfield Beach, Florida

www.hci-online.com

Library of Congress Cataloging-in-Publication Data

Adamse, Michael, date.
    Anniversary : a love story / Michael Adamse.
        p.   cm.
    ISBN 1-55874-542-4 (pbk.)
    I. Title.
PS3551.D39537A82   1998   97-32582
813'.54—dc21   CIP

Publisher: Health Communications, Inc.
               3201 S.W. 15th Street
               Deerfield Beach, Florida 33442-8190

Cover design by Lawna Patterson Oldfield
Cover photo ©1998 SuperStock, Inc.

Anniversary
is dedicated with love
to my wife,
Diane Elise Leeds

Acknowledgments

nniversary was written with the help and inspiration of many other people. It is my pleasure to be able to thank several of them now in print.

I am sincerely grateful to my publishers, Peter Vegso and Gary Seidler, who have given me the opportunity to fulfill a lifelong dream of writing. Their faith in me and their vision toward the future are deeply appreciated.

My senior editor and friend, Matthew Diener, deserves my deepest thanks and admiration. His guidance and push for excellence have helped me greatly. Thank you, Matthew.

Thank you also to Erica Orloff, whose editing skills and insights were very helpful. I want to express my appreciation to all the staff at Health Communications for their ongoing support, especially Christine Belleris, Allison Janse and Lisa

v

Drucker in the editorial department. Thanks as well to Ronni O'Brien and Kim Weiss for their publicity efforts and for showing me the ins and outs of working with the media. My appreciation also goes to Kelly Johnson Maragni, Irene Xanthos, Randee Goldsmith, Yvonne zum Tobel and the rest of the sales/marketing team for promoting the book.

Thanks to Engel and Maria Adamse, my parents, for their support, and to my sisters and brother, Maria, Marina, Yvonne, Camilla and Frank.

I want to express my appreciation also to Karen, Steve, Sammy and Max Yellen; Rebecca Radzivill; Diana Kenney; Cindy and Sam Lebovic; Joan, John, Kelly and Sara Sparks; and Don Campagna, whose friendship and enthusiasm have meant a great deal to me. Thank you to my friends Richard and Barry Wright; Joel Sands; Paul Bessette; and the Kamensteins—Carol, David, Tracy and Sloan.

A special note of appreciation to my lifelong best friend, Jerry "JC" Smith, for always showing me his interest and excitement. If you are blessed in life with one friend like Jerry, then you can truly count yourself as fortunate.

To my daughters, Elise and Dana, I want you to know how much I appreciate your interest in my writing and your patience while I was glued for hours to the keyboard.

Ground Zero

Richard felt the softness of his wife's skin against his fingers as he ran his hand slowly over her back and shoulders. Laura was lying on her stomach, blond hair flowing and draped over her shoulders. Her head was turned sideways and she rested her cheek on her folded hands. Her eyes were closed and there was a peaceful look on her face.

Richard knelt down and gently buried his face in her curls, taking in the scent of her freshly washed hair.

Not a word was spoken as he turned her over. His lips moved to hers and they began to kiss. Slowly at first.

Restraint soon gave way to pure passion.

Richard and Laura's bodies were taking over, and the basic chemistry that had pulled them together so many years ago found its rhythm.

There was no outside world. Just the two of them.

The ringing phone seemed so far off at first. He wanted to ignore it, but it was getting louder and louder.

Richard's eyes opened slowly and he looked across the void where Laura should have been and noticed the clock: 3:17 A.M.

He fumbled for the receiver, but even in his half-awake state he noticed right away that his heart was beginning to race. It was as though his body knew something before his mind did.

"Hello?" The anxiety was already present in his voice.

Richard heard his father's trembling voice on the other end. "Your mom died a few minutes ago. It's over, son."

The words hit him like a sledgehammer. Richard had always been close to his mother, and he felt waves of anguish overwhelm him.

He found no solace in the fact that she wasn't in pain anymore.

He struggled to orient himself and to think of something comforting to say. But what could he really say to his father that would change anything or make it better? Still, the words came out automatically. "Oh God, Dad. I'm so sorry."

His father responded immediately. Voice cracking, he explained, "I told them not to try to resuscitate her, Richard. That was what she wanted." A short pause. "I really can't talk right now." Richard sensed his father was about to cry.

Something inside him expected his father to be strong, to somehow protect his son from feeling the pain of his own loss, even after losing his wife of forty-nine years.

"Okay, Dad. I'll get there as soon as possible."

They both hung up and Richard stared straight ahead, filled with a sense of numbing disbelief. He didn't cry. He hadn't been able to cry for some time now, even though at times he'd wanted to.

He felt desperately alone and, despite the fact that they had separated six months ago, Richard automatically reached to pick up the phone and call his wife. He wanted more than anything to have Laura hold him close. Richard had moved only a couple of miles up the road and knew he could be with her in a matter of minutes.

He had told himself he wanted to live close enough to make things convenient for the children. Richard's psychiatrist, Dr. Allison, thought differently. She'd made an interesting comment in a recent session.

"Well, Richard, I sense that you chose your apartment for another reason entirely." She said it softly but in an assured manner that communicated she spoke the truth. Richard knew from past experience that this was the tone she used when she was about to say something he did not want to admit.

"Okay, I'll bite. What's your interpretation?"

"I think you've moved closer to your family in an unconscious effort to be connected to Laura. It's related to your difficulty in letting go."

Dr. Allison added something else. "And it's entirely understandable. It's hard to go through a divorce." She was a kind and compassionate therapist who understood the complexities of life.

"That's my interpretation of what you're doing, but I think you need to protect yourself better. You may want to consider moving a little farther away so you're less likely to run into her."

Richard never had admitted it, but he knew his therapist was right. He put the phone down. He'd have to get used to living without her, even at a time like this.

Richard still loved Laura. He knew that. But their marriage had been in a downward spiral for several years now. They had so many problems.

Before they separated, Richard had sometimes made a mental list of them. Their marriage lacked affection and intimacy. Their sex life was almost nonexistent, and when they did make love it was mechanical. They both had demanding careers and different interests.

Then, too, a thousand things annoyed each about the other. These were trivial at face value but related to the deeper problem that they just no longer connected. She was always punctual, and he was guaranteed to be at least fifteen minutes late. She thought that flossing in front of him was fine, while he found it disgusting. He wanted to smoke an occasional cigar when they went out. She hated it. He squeezed the toothpaste from the center. She squeezed it from the end.

The fighting finally had taken its toll on both of them and they were about to become another statistic, some demographic obscurity. Their children would come from a household with divorced parents. Perhaps they even would go on to *blend* with another family if he or Laura married again. Friends told him the children would be better off living in a household without the tension and conflict, but he never believed it.

Life really sucks, he thought. *It's like a building falling in on itself. And when it comes down, it all seems to come down at once. You lose your mother and your wife all in the same year.*

He was at ground zero of an exploding bomb marked "despair."

He had no time to be despondent now. His father needed him. Richard tried to pull himself together the best he could and booked a flight to San Francisco. He poured a stiff drink and began calling his sisters to see how they were doing. It was going to be a long night.

"Hi, Marcia. It's Richard."

"Hi, Richard. How are you doing?" The upbeat tone of her voice made him realize that she hadn't heard the news yet. Richard wasn't prepared for that. He'd just assumed that, as the youngest child, he'd hear it last.

He looked at the clock: 3:57 A.M. It was 8:57 A.M. in London now, so Marcia was awake. She probably didn't realize the time difference at first. If she had, she would have known her brother wasn't making a social call at this time of night.

"Did Dad call you about Mom?" In a nanosecond he entertained the fantasy that she already knew, but that was impossible.

"No." There was a pause. "Oh God, what?" Marcia's tone of voice became anxious and tense, revealing that she anticipated what was coming next.

"I'm sorry. I thought he called you already. She died an hour or so ago."

There. It was out. He took a strong sip of the straight vodka he'd poured just minutes before.

"Oh God, Richard. How's Dad?"

He knew Marcia so well. She was putting her own feelings aside, as she'd always done.

"I don't know. He got off the phone pretty fast." Richard quickly asked, "What should we do about Marie and Suzanne? You want to split them up?"

As soon as he said it he realized how stupid that sounded. "I mean you call one and I call the other?" Richard corrected himself.

"I know what you meant." There was a short pause on the other end. Marcia needed to catch her breath. She was about to take charge. He was counting on it. "All right, Richard. I'll call Marie and you call Suzanne. Then we'll call each other back. I'll check in with Dad first though."

"Okay, Marcia. I love you."

"I love you too, Richard." They had grown used to saying that at the end of each phone call during Marcia's own bout with cancer. Though she had survived, they both realized that they had no time to waste.

As Richard dialed Suzanne's number, he hoped that she had already heard from Dad. She picked up on the first ring.

"Hi, Richard. Damn." She was crying. Suzanne knew.

"How did you know it was me?"

"Caller ID. How did Dad sound to you?"

"I didn't talk to him long. You know Dad. He's not about to let any of us know. I'm headed out tomorrow morning. How about you?"

"As soon as I can get there. I knew it was coming but there was no way I could have known how it would feel. I hate it." It was hard to make out Suzanne's words through her weeping.

At that moment, Richard felt his own guard slipping and he began to cry. He didn't need to be a therapist now. He allowed himself to be a son and a brother.

"Call me anytime, Suzanne."

"You too, Richard."

With that acknowledgment they both hung up. Neither of them felt like saying anything more right now.

Richard poured himself another drink. He looked out the window over the Miami skyline and decided he'd had enough for one night. He walked into the bathroom to retrieve a ten-milligram tablet of Ambien that Dr. Allison had prescribed to help him sleep. He read the warning on the side: "May cause drowsiness. Alcohol may intensify this effect."

"Good," Richard said out loud. "I'm counting on it." Thirty minutes later he was sound asleep.

The flight from Miami to San Francisco left early the next morning. Before getting on the plane, he left a message on Laura's voice mail at work. It was short and to the point. He wasn't ready to deal with her directly right now.

In a flat monotone Richard said, "My mother died last night. I'm on my way to see my father. Tell the girls I love them and I'll call them tonight. You know where to reach me." It was a calculated tone of voice meant to reveal no emotion.

Richard was glad he hadn't given in to calling her last night. His defenses were back up and he wasn't about to share any feelings with her. If she felt some guilt over not being there for him, so much the better.

As the flight turned west from Miami, Richard looked out the window. He could see the sparkling morning light reflecting off the marsh and pools of water that characterized the Everglades. It was primordial, mysterious and strangely beautiful. Had he been on this flight for any other purpose, he could have savored this moment.

He and his sisters had planned to get together for their parents' fiftieth anniversary, not for this. His twin sisters,

Marie and Marcia, would fly in the next day.

Richard thought about how Marie and Marcia's relationship with their mother had been strained at times, especially during adolescence.

He recalled one incident in particular detail. It took place in the sixties, when the twins were around sixteen. They were both getting ready to go out on a double date. His father was out of town and his mom wasn't thrilled with the way the girls were dressed.

"It's as simple as this. Neither of you is going out like that." His mother said with a strong air of authority.

"Like what?" Marcia responded with irritation.

"You know what I mean. Your skirts are too short."

"Get with it, Mom," Marie chimed in to support her sister.

"No, *you* get with it," his mother yelled. "Go change or cancel your date."

As he recalled, the fight went on like that for some time. The only other part Richard remembered was coming to his sisters' defense by relaying to his mother that all the girls at school dressed that way. None of the arguing helped. The twins ended up changing and left in a huff.

Thinking back, he had to admit that they looked provocative in those outfits. Objectively, he knew his twin sisters were very attractive. They had long, wavy red hair and deep blue eyes that testified to their Irish heritage. Even his friends would make comments now and again about how pretty they looked.

After they were both married and had their own children, they grew closer to their mother. They came to appreciate the stresses of motherhood. The same was true for his other sister, Suzanne. She and their mother got along best after Suzanne started her own family.

Looking back at the time, Richard could see that, compared with today, the conflicts his three sisters had experienced with his mother were pretty lightweight, more a rite of passage that children went through with their same-sex parents than anything else.

At least his sisters could all take some comfort in the knowledge that their relationships with their mother were solid ones when she died. As far as he knew, there weren't any major emotional loose ends for them to contend with now.

Unlike his sisters, he never really went through a tough time with his mother. Perhaps it was being the only son. It afforded him a special status in the family. Of course, being the youngest didn't hurt, either.

He remembered the day he began kindergarten. Scared to leave the comfort of family and friends and be in a classroom full of strangers, that first day of school he had hidden.

He told Laura once that he must have intuitively known at the age of five that kindergarten signaled the beginning of a life full of responsibilities. He smiled weakly when he thought about how much they had laughed at that. Not because it was funny, but because it was true.

His mother had found him and then had calmly walked him to his classroom, reassuring him that everything would be all right. She had promised to be there to pick him up at the end of the day. He had looked out the window for what seemed like the whole day, waiting and watching for her return. When the school day finally did end, she had greeted him with a handful of cookies.

Richard now wished he'd shared that memory with his mother to see if she would have remembered it. She probably would have, considering she had always recalled everything else. Whenever he asked her a detailed question about any of their childhoods, she immediately knew the answer.

He remembered how his mother had carefully placed a quarter in a folded paper napkin every morning before school. It was her ritual to wrap his school lunch money in a napkin. Richard never understood why his mother needed to wrap his lunch money, until lunch became more expensive and he needed a nickel as well as a quarter.

He also recalled the time she had surprised him with a birthday party when he was eleven. She had gone all out: his favorite chocolate cake, all his friends. He remembered how happy he was and wished he could go back there now, back in time to when he was eleven and everything was simpler. All he had worried about was whether or not there'd be any cake left over for a second piece. Life would never be that uncomplicated again.

His mother had been a wonderful, nurturing person. His father was going to have a hard time adjusting. Richard felt a deep sadness. His parents had always enjoyed a great marriage. Richard could barely remember them arguing at all. On occasion he even asked them directly if there were ever any difficulties, and they always answered no.

"Life was much simpler before," his mother always said. Richard pressed on. "You mean with four kids you never had problems?"

"Not really," his father answered.

Richard found that difficult to believe. Maybe they just dealt with their problems better.

In truth, Richard felt somewhat jealous of his parents'

marriage. They had shown each other so much devotion and affection. They had held hands and kissed. He could remember his father reaching around his mother's waist as she leaned over the stove to make dinner. Why couldn't his own marriage have been more like that?

After Richard's children were born, his marriage had changed. He and Laura made love less frequently. Eventually, it became a sexless marriage with barely any touching. He couldn't remember the last time he reached around Laura's waist to hold her close. Toward the end, just before they separated, he still occasionally tried to be affectionate with her, but Laura always just sighed and stiffened, her defenses up in a fraction of a second. After a while, he just gave up.

He also recalled how his parents had talked all the time. With all their responsibilities, they had taken time for each other. He could still see them in his mind's eye, sitting in the kitchen every morning before his father went off to work. She made the coffee and they talked about the upcoming day's events. At the end of the day, they sat together and talked some more. He couldn't for the life of him remember about what, but that wasn't important. They were truly devoted to each other; they were committed to the family and all that came with it.

Richard secretly felt like a failure. With all his years of training as a psychiatrist, he believed he should know, more than most, how to make a relationship work. Why couldn't he have a marriage like his parents'? And Richard had only two children, not four.

What was his excuse? Based on his training, he knew that he might be distorting these childhood memories as selective memory or wishful thinking. But the more he thought, the more he realized that his parents had a great marriage. They relied on each other to work out whatever conflicts they had. They had no self-help books or marriage encounters to turn to for help, no slick infomercials that promised to save your relationship in ten easy installments.

Richard concluded that they enjoyed one distinct advantage over him and Laura. They lived most of their married life during an easier time and didn't experience the same pressures of modern-day life. His parents' demands were mostly external, not internal like his and Laura's. His father and mother were concerned themselves with outside forces that applied pressure. Bills, child rearing and fatigue were definitely stressful by themselves. He realized they must have had difficult moments. Moments perhaps, but certainly not difficult years. Maybe it wasn't that they had it easier. Life was hard during most of their married years, but it was also less complicated.

His and Laura's problems went much deeper. They thought and communicated in fundamentally different ways. He tended to be more emotional and lived in a perpetual gray zone of life's unanswered questions. She tended to be more logical and linear in her approach to life. Laura was decisive and saw the world in monochrome. They used to laugh about how she thought more traditionally like a man, and he more like a woman. As time went on that became less funny.

To make matters even worse, this was his second marriage. No one else in the family had ever divorced. In truth, Richard hurt deeply because he had failed twice at the most fundamental commitment in his life.

Richard wished he could turn his mind off, but that would never happen. Perhaps it was an occupational hazard, this preoccupation with relationships and the way in which they worked—or in his case, didn't work. If he was awake, he'd be thinking. That's just the way it was.

He closed his eyes and thought he'd take a break for a moment or two. Less than five minutes later, he was fast asleep.

The announcement that the plane would be landing shortly interrupted Richard's respite. He looked at his watch and realized that he'd slept for almost three hours. He had needed the rest and was grateful for that.

He went to the bathroom to freshen up before they landed and looked into the small mirror, studying his reflection for a moment. His full head of brown hair was showing more than a hint of gray on the sides now. Richard felt as though he'd aged quite a bit over the past several months. He looked deep into his own blue eyes staring back at him and wished he were on a flight to nowhere, rather than where he really was.

Richard took a paper towel, wet it with cold water and ran it over his face. He took a deep breath and returned to his seat.

Richard knew his father would come to the airport to pick him up. That wasn't unusual. Half the time his mother had come to the airport with his father, while the other half she'd stayed at the house preparing a meal. But when he and his father got back to the house today, she wouldn't be there. Seeing his father alone would take some getting used to on his part. But Richard knew his own adjustments would be easy compared with his father's. After all these years of marriage, his father would now be by himself.

Richard planned to stay a few days to help his dad sort out his affairs, but then he'd return home. He knew his sisters would need to get back to their own families also. It was hard living so far away, but that was the reality.

The plane landed smoothly, and as he walked through the jetway his heart beat faster with fear and anticipation. For a split second, he felt as though he were five years old again on the first day of school. Only now, he couldn't afford to show his fear. He didn't need to add any burdens to his father's grief.

It wouldn't hurt to have a shot of courage right now.

Just then, Richard recalled the words Laura had spoken in the intensive care unit when their younger daughter's heart was failing. Sandi had made it through all right, but they hadn't known at the time how it would turn out.

"Right now, this is about what *she* needs, not us. We have to be strong for her," Laura had said.

It was one of her simple black and white, matter-of-fact statements. Laura hadn't meant to be insensitive. She just had been helping them both focus on what they needed to do at the moment. He remembered how tired and pale Laura had looked, but as frightened as she had been, she had taken charge.

One of the things he admired most about Laura was her strength. She was tough, and it was an aspect of her personality that he loved but sometimes hated at the same time. He loved it when she used it on their behalf, and hated it when she used it to defend herself.

The jetway was backed up, and it gave Richard a moment to remember one of the last fights he had with Laura while they were still living together. They had been arguing about what he saw as her complete lack of affection. They'd had this fight many times.

It started when Richard turned over in bed and began rubbing her shoulders. This was the first physical contact of any kind between the two of them in weeks. The children were fast asleep and it was late at night.

Laura firmly pushed his hands away. "I'm tired, Richard," she said in a neutral voice, not aggressive but certainly not inviting.

"What else is new? You're always tired."

Laura wasn't about to let that go. "Back off, Richard. I'm tired and our marriage is falling apart. What do you expect? We're on the verge of a divorce!"

Her voice grew louder. "Do you think I'm going to risk being close to you even for a second? Just so we can have another argument after I let my guard down? Forget it."

Richard got out of bed and made his way to the living room couch, as he'd done many other times. Before slamming the door shut, he paused to get in one more barb. "*You* let your guard down and be soft?" The sarcasm was unmistakable. "I'd have to be an idiot to have that fantasy."

That particular time Laura did not follow him out to continue the fight, as she had done in the past.

Richard had heard her sobbing though the closed door. He wished he hadn't. He had grown too sick and tired of the whole situation to give her any comfort. He thought on several occasions afterward that if he could go back in time, he would have gone back in and held her. But that opportunity would never come again.

He was nearing the end of the jetway now and turned the final corner that led into the terminal.

Richard needed to get out of his own head for now, and Laura's words about Sandi helped him. It was his father who had lost his wife of forty-nine years to cancer, not he. The cancer had stolen his mother away, and there was nothing his father could have done to stop it. No choice he could have made would have changed the result. Richard's situation was different.

Losing Laura was a choice.

When his father came into view, Richard felt a sense of much-needed power and courage surge through his veins.

Anniversary

A light drizzle fell on those who had gathered to bury Sarah. The sweet smell of freshly cut grass filled the late afternoon air, while a slight breeze rustled the oak branches overhead.

Richard looked around and guessed that there were over a hundred people there. He was half listening to the eulogy as his eyes fell on his three sisters standing across from him. Marie and Marcia still looked so much alike after all these years. Their red hair, blue eyes and light complexions provided a sharp contrast to the black dresses they were wearing. He thought back to when they were children and all the times they had worn the same clothes and fooled everyone who couldn't tell them apart. Everyone, that is, except him. Now, Marie had a short, chic haircut, while

Marcia still wore hers past her shoulders. Their taste in clothes had evolved too. Maybe it was part of each of them becoming her own person and not just being a twin.

Suzanne stood next to them. Her blond hair reminded him of Laura's. Her normally thin face with its high cheekbones was puffy now, swollen by the many hours she had spent crying over the woman they all desperately missed. Suzanne considered her mother one of her best friends.

Then there was his father. His gray hair and hazel eyes still showed him to be a handsome man. Christopher stood without moving at all, quiet and stoic as Richard expected he would be.

Richard wondered what his father was thinking, standing in the cemetery and saying good-bye to his wife after forty-nine years of marriage. He quickly concluded it was something he would never know.

After the funeral, everyone returned home one by one and went back to their lives. Richard was the last to leave. His dad had declined Marcia's offer to move in with her. He had too many friends in San Francisco and had lived there for more than twenty years. He didn't want any more changes.

The night before Richard's flight back to Miami his father asked, "Richard, how are you and Laura doing? I mean with the divorce." He asked the question in a quiet and deliberate tone of voice, his eyes riveted on Richard.

"All right, Dad. Things are moving ahead." It was a response that was more perfunctory than anything else. How could everything be "all right"?

Richard didn't fool his father, who persisted. "No, I mean it, son. How are you?"

"Look, Dad, now is not the time."

His father answered right away. "Now *is* the time. When do we get the chance to really talk? I want to know." Richard hesitated for just a second and then it all came out.

"Laura is wrapped up in the kids and her work. She isn't interested in me. I don't need a lot of attention but I do need some.

"I'm unappreciated and taken for granted. She's got it good and doesn't realize it. And worst of all, there's no affection from her and our sex life has been over for a long time."

Richard caught his breath before continuing, "I try, Dad. I know she's not the only one to blame. I'm more sophisticated than that. I deal with it all day long. I know what the complaints are. I hear about the husbands who are too wrapped up in sports or whatever.

"Hell, Dad, I'm a guy who can actually talk about feelings. I need someone who is warmer and can give up ground now and again. I should have known when I married a lawyer that it meant she would never admit she was wrong."

Richard talked for a good hour or so, and afterward he felt guilty. His father had listened carefully but hadn't offered any encouraging words. It wasn't unlike him. He tended to keep his personal thoughts to himself. It was hard to tell what went on in his head. But you could see the wheels turning.

After such a long marriage, Richard hoped his father would have had some words of wisdom to offer. It was asking too much a week after his mother's death. The night ended when Richard finished complaining.

"Well, son, I hope things work out for the best." His father rose slowly from the chair opposite the one his mother had sat in for many years. "You've got an early flight out tomorrow. Get some rest. I'll see you in the morning."

Richard went upstairs to bed and stared at the ceiling. He was looking forward to getting on the plane and returning home after spending the time at his father's. He wished he'd wake up the next morning and find out he'd been dreaming. His mother would have the coffee going and he'd head home to Laura and the children, who would eagerly greet him in Miami. *Keep dreaming*, Richard said to himself as he finally drifted off to sleep.

Early the next morning, he and his father left for the airport. The ride was somber and quiet.

The terminal was crowded and they waited anxiously at the gate. The final boarding call signaled the need to say goodbye. Richard wondered whether this was the last time he'd see his father alive. His dad was in good health but he knew that spouses often die soon after losing their partners. He'd seen it enough in his work. It was all a bit much to handle. His father hugged him tightly and whispered, " I love you, son."

Richard returned the embrace. " I love you too, Dad." Just as he turned to leave, his father touched Richard's shoulder and said, "Hold on a second." He reached inside his coat pocket and pulled out a thick envelope sealed with tape and marked simply in his handwriting "For Richard."

Before he had a chance to ask, his father instructed him, "Open this up on the plane. It's a very special gift. I think it will beat the movie or any in-flight magazine." He smiled weakly and turned away.

Richard wondered what contents the envelope held. He boarded the plane, found his seat, settled in and opened the package. He discovered a fresh sheet of bond paper clipped to the first of many letters in a stack.

He immediately recognized the handwriting on the letters as both his father's and mother's. The ones in his father's handwriting were originals, while those in his mother's were copies. Richard wondered when his dad had found the time to make copies during this crazy week. These must be very important documents.

At first glance, it looked like the letters alternated between those of his father and mother. Many of his father's letters were obviously weathered by age.

With a sense of disbelief and curiosity, he began reading the cover letter.

My dearest son Richard,

What you will find here is a collection of personal letters between your mother and me. There is nothing that I value more now that she's gone.

These letters represent a sample of what I wrote to your mother on every anniversary of our marriage. It was a tradition I started on our first anniversary, and during the course of our marriage, I never missed a year. I didn't have the intention of sharing these with you or anyone else. They are very private and reflect my most intimate feelings.

My generation never shared with sons or daughters anything about their marriages. I believe you can understand that. I haven't decided whether or not this is one advantage your generation has over mine. Everything these days seems to come out in the open all the time. We never dreamt of sharing what today becomes public on the talk shows for millions of strangers to see. I really believe that some things should be kept private.

I'm sharing these letters with you now because I love both you and Laura and because I love my grandchildren. In my heart, I believe you will find strength in these words and hope between the lines.

I suppose your mother and I were a little unusual for our generation. We actually talked about feelings. We struggled quite a bit, as you will see. But we never wavered in our mission to raise a family of loved children. There were times of doubt, but we never lost faith in each other.

You've asked at times if we'd ever had problems. We never acknowledged to you that we did. We both believed in keeping these matters between ourselves. Your grandparents never shared any of their personal matters with us.

I feel differently now that your mother is gone.

As I've said, I've given you a sample of letters that reflect some of the changes we went through over the years. There is no reason for you to have all of them. The rest will remain forever between your mother and me.

These letters are very difficult to share with you now, but my love for you is greater than any need to preserve my pride about these matters. I only ask that you keep the secret of these letters to yourself. I am trusting that you will not think any less of me after reading them, as I am imperfect like all of us.

Contrary to what you may be thinking, Richard, you haven't failed in your relationships. You simply need help understanding the bigger picture. You're reading these letters because that's what I believe will help you. Had I felt that any of your sisters needed to read them, I would have done the same.

There is one more thing I'd like you to know. I found your mother's diary among her belongings shortly after her death. I did not know of its existence until I discovered it, but I know she wanted me to find it, as you will read for yourself in her last letter. Her diary contains many entries over the years. I found it interesting that my anniversary letters were always followed by one of her own.

There were many things that I knew because we talked quite a bit during our later years, after all of you were grown. Some things were hurtful and others completely surprised me. You have my original letters and copies of your mother's, which I wish to read again and again from the pages she wrote in her own hand.

I am not bothered by her need to keep these letters private. Your mother was and will always remain the love of my life. We had a good life together and I miss her terribly.

Our life was far more rich than it was poor. Perhaps the hard times are what made the great times seem so wonderful.

Marriage is often very hard, Richard. Love is hard. Sometimes it's much more difficult to stay than leave. Someone told me once that the measure of love was how much you'd be willing to give up for it. I never forgot that.

There are good times . . . and bad ones, too. It's not a cliché. It is reality. Your mother and I always respected each other, and even when it would have been much easier to leave, we both stayed. Leaving wasn't part of our culture. Commitment was.

Marriage and parenthood taught me that the secret of love is being selfless. The words are simple, but if you follow them, they will prove themselves true. Try to remember that. Forty-nine years seems like such a long time when you say the words. Believe me, they're over in a heartbeat.

My hope is that you and Laura find it within yourselves to work out your differences. Whatever you decide, I love you both and the children.

Dad

Richard reread the letter more slowly. It hadn't sunk in completely the first time. He realized it was a question of form versus content. He understood the content; the words and their meaning were clear enough. It was the form that he struggled to accept.

His father wrote these words. It would take some time for that to register.

He'd always thought of his parents in that certain way children do. They were one-dimensional. Dad and Mom. Not Christopher and Sarah. He couldn't help feeling that he was about to become something of a thief: a burglar stealing the deepest secrets of his parents' marriage. He thought for a moment about when he had discovered the copies of *Playboy* under his dad's mattress. That had been bad enough.

Richard had been fourteen years old at that time. His puberty had been in full swing, and his curiosity about girls and their anatomy had become an adolescent preoccupation. Sex had been constantly on his mind and the minds of most of his friends.

His dad and mom had gone out somewhere and he had sneaked into their room for a few minutes. His friend David had been with him.

David had shown Richard his own father's girlie magazine collection, so it was up to Richard to reciprocate. He had suspected that there might be something under the mattress. He'd seen his dad put something under there once, and he was sure it wasn't *Reader's Digest*.

"Wow, David, look at this!" He had felt a mixture of excitement and guilt at finding two copies of *Playboy*. After all, he had invaded the sanctity of his parents' bedroom. For a well-trained Catholic boy of fourteen, the act had necessarily involved his conscience. Still, adolescent lust had overtaken moral principle for the moment.

"Have you ever seen breasts like that?" Richard, wide-eyed, had asked his friend.

"What a body," David had responded. "You know something, Richard, we're two men of the world."

"That we are, David. That we are."

But this was altogether different. His father was extending him an invitation to see the inner workings of his parents' marriage. He would be peering into the most private thoughts of his own parents' minds. That was far more intimate than looking at some *Playboy* magazines. It felt wrong somehow, even though he had his dad's permission. Yet it was more than that.

His father *wanted* him to read it. Part of Richard resisted the desire to turn the page. He wanted to preserve the myth. He didn't want to know about the problems or the conflicts. He wanted to stay a child in relation to his parents. Still, as his father had just explained, he wasn't sharing these letters lightly. There was a greater purpose, one that overrode any need to preserve childhood innocence.

Richard took a deep breath and turned the page.

Year One

The paper that he held in his hand was weathered and yellowed with age. Richard realized that these words had been penned some forty-nine years ago, almost eight years before he was even born. His father was twenty-two years old at the time, and his mother twenty-one. It was like traveling through a time warp.

Richard handled the letters gently. They were a piece of history that deserved respect. He slowly began reading one of his father's letters.

Dearest Sarah,

On this, our first wedding anniversary, there are some things I would like you to know.

Know this, Sarah . . .

I love you more deeply with each passing day. I feel like a man who has found a treasure. Not jewels or material goods of any kind, but the riches a man can only pray he will experience in his lifetime. A love that no king can buy.

Know this, Sarah . . .

I savor every minute we make love, and how you fall asleep in my arms afterward. Remember how we had to sneak into your room at night, fearful that your parents might catch us? What a pleasure it is to freely feel you close to me. To caress your hair. To feel the gentleness of your skin against mine. To move my hands over every curve of your body. My passion for you is overwhelming.

Know this, Sarah . . .

I admire you both openly and secretly. I admire your intelligence. I admire your strength.

Know this, Sarah . . .

I feel truly blessed to have found you. I will never take you for granted. Our family will be happy and strengthened by the bond that you and I have. We will be the core around which our children grow—physically, spiritually and emotionally.

Know this, Sarah . . .

There will be no obstacles in our life than we cannot overcome together as a team. Husband and wife . . . and soon, father and mother.

Know this above all, Sarah . . .

I love you now and forever,
Christopher

He'd never known his father to be like this.

Richard never thought of his father as romantic. He knew he was devoted and loving to his wife and children. That was always clear. But a romantic side was something he'd never seen, until just now.

Richard remembered the love letters he and Laura had exchanged when they first dated. Now he thought they were syrupy and naive. Real relationships never stayed that way. The reality of work, children and schedules tempered them. The innocence of young love doesn't survive very long.

The reality of his parents actually having sex with each other before they got married astounded him. He couldn't believe his father was sharing this with him. He now realized that, of course, his parents had felt the overwhelming passion and lust of youth, just as he had.

He now wondered if his parents had known that he and his first girlfriend sometimes had sex downstairs on the family room couch while everyone was home. Richard now identified with his father—he knew that being afraid that your parents might catch you could certainly cramp your romantic style. Of course, he realized this letter was from the early years of their marriage.

Richard was curious to see what his mother felt at the end of their first year of marriage together. He knew that it would be full of love and devotion, as would the letters from later years. She was a kind woman who had a soft heart. Strong but not tough.

Why couldn't Laura have been more like her? *If she had,* he thought, *we wouldn't be getting a divorce this month.*

Richard realized that he was a part of the problem. He

knew that he could improve things about himself, but he just could no longer tolerate Laura's failure to appreciate him. She neglected his needs. She was totally caught up in the children and her career, and he was tired of being last on her list. Maybe if he'd been given these letters some months ago, his father would have given him permission to show them to Laura. Then perhaps she would have learned the correct way to treat a partner. It was too late now.

Dear Christopher,

I love you dearly. This has been a magical year for us. I feel like the happiest woman in the world. You are everything I ever wanted in a man. Strong and masculine. Sensitive and romantic. I know that when we start our family together, you will be a wonderful father.

You know that I am a private person. My feelings are hard to share. I feel somewhat split right now. A piece of me wishes to share this letter with you, but I have been trained well. My mother always taught me that a woman must keep much of what she feels inside, even when a voice within screams to let it out.

Not because "it's a man's world," as some of our contemporaries like to think. Rather, it's because a woman is the glue that holds a family together. Providing this bond carries with it an enormous responsibility, part of which is to be silent. I don't know if that's right or wrong.

I do know that the future holds many unknowns. Responsibilities will challenge us in many ways. But what will never be threatened are our love and undying commitment. I know this, not because I am wise beyond my years, but because my mother sat me down the night before you and I were married.

She simply let me know that there would be good times and bad times, but that our love for each other would see us through anything and everything.

I feel prepared for and even welcome all that may come in the future.

Christopher, I love and cherish you more than I ever have anyone else.

Darling, I'm yours forever,
Sarah

It wasn't what he expected. Richard realized that his mother was a lot more sophisticated than he ever had given her credit for being. She was both romantic and realistic. He felt that she somehow knew there would be hard times ahead. In comparison, his father's letter was romantic but naive.

He now knew these letters would change his view of his parents forever. In the course of one brief reading, Richard could already see that his parents led much fuller lives than he had ever imagined. This was going to be interesting in-flight reading all right.

At once, a hundred thoughts and questions went through his mind. His parents actually had a life before children. What had it been like? And these letters, how had they exchanged them? Did his father give them to his mother to read privately, or had she read them in front of him? And what of her responses?

Why hadn't she given this or any of the other anniversary letters to him to read? Was it really just that she wanted to have her own special place to record her thoughts and feelings? Her words didn't seem as though they contained anything she couldn't share.

There were many details about these letters that he wanted to know. For now, though, it really didn't matter. He knew where his father was going with this and appreciated what he was trying to do.

Dad wanted him to reconsider. Richard didn't need to read all of the anniversary letters to figure that out. Besides, he'd said as much in his cover letter. Richard thought, *Your life with Mom and mine with Laura are like apples and oranges; another world, another time.*

"I'll read the letters, Dad, but it's not going to work," Richard said out loud.

Year Three

efore Richard even read the next pair of anniversary letters, he knew it had been a big year in his parents' lives. He was very curious about what they would have to say about it.

His twin sisters had been born in year three, after barely two years of marriage. Their birth was a pivotal event considering that another three children would be born over the next five years.

Richard wondered if either of his parents knew just how dramatically it would forever change their marriage. It was a fact of life that becoming a parent was like joining a secret club. Outsiders had no idea what it was like to be a member until they joined. You could observe, listen and surmise from the outside, but nothing really prepared you.

And yet, Richard thought that perhaps there was something wrong with him. He loved his children, but his own parents seemed so much better at parenting, so selfless and devoted. It wasn't as though Richard didn't feel the initial wonder of the birth of his very own flesh and blood. He did. He remembered his first daughter's birth. He and Laura had wept and kissed each other passionately when they heard that first cry.

But Richard had concluded that for him being a parent was a mixture of privilege and never-ending responsibility; responsibility for both the physical and, more important, the emotional welfare of his two girls. He often thought that because he was a parent of small children he had no choice but to place his own life and his marriage on hold. And to a very large extent, that was true.

When he was honest with himself, he knew that, even though he was more involved than most fathers, Laura had it even worse. She had a busy career and bore the bulk of the responsibility for the children. She took the kids to the doctor, helped with their homework and attended to all the family's household needs. Laura sat down with Sandi every night and discussed the day. When Christa had to cram for a last-minute spelling test, it was Laura who got up early to quiz her.

But Richard would never admit all this to Laura lest she use it against him. This was one of the dynamics of their relationship. He saw admitting things to her as a double-edged sword—she could later use any of his admissions as ammunition. This would help solidify her belief that she was always right, and he wasn't about to help her do that.

Time to read what his dad had to say back in 1951.

Dear Sarah,

Happy anniversary, "Mom." I am so thrilled this year.
What a wonderful surprise to be blessed with twins. When
the doctor came into the waiting room with the news, I was
ecstatic. When Dr. Thomas said the words "twin girls,"
I felt tears well up in my eyes.

Racing down to your room, I was the happiest man in the
world. I couldn't wait for the elevator and ran up the five
flights of stairs, out of breath, finding my way to your room.
But I must tell you, it was a mixture of excitement and
nervousness. I didn't know what to expect and thought about
just how helpless and fragile they would be.

I knew the babies would be isolated for some time before
I could touch them. But at least I wanted to see my girls
through the glass of the nursery. Minutes felt like hours
and, when I finally arrived, I saw a nurse who turned the
twins toward me with a smile as if to say, "Here's another
anxious father." Marie was crying, while Marcia seemed
to be looking up at the light overhead contentedly, almost
seriously. I speculated, <u>Would this be their personalities?</u>

I knew this was routine for the nurse, but for me there was
nothing routine about it. I was experiencing feelings that I
never had before and never knew I was capable of.

Remember how nervous we were when we first brought
them home after the week in the hospital? I was afraid of so
many things. But, Sarah, I must tell you that you were a
natural. I was so proud of you.

But at the same time, I felt some sadness: I was sorry that Dad wasn't here to enjoy them. I know how happy the twins would have made him. Still, I took some comfort in seeing the joy in your parents' eyes.

What a strange and awesome experience that must be, to see your own child now a mother of your first grandchildren. God willing, we will see such a day as well.

For now, we have a mission ahead of us, don't we, honey? We are entrusted with raising our children to be happy, healthy, strong and respectful of others. That should keep us well occupied for the next twenty years or so.

Already I can see that being a parent will hold special challenges for us. We never would have imagined functioning on only four hours of sleep a night. Well, I trust that will change soon enough.

I have found that I appreciate what our own parents went through. They had it even tougher than we do. They had so many fewer conveniences. But we both know that material goods are so much less important than a strong foundation of love.

Our parents were not perfect, but they did love us, and that came through. I suspect it's hard to raise a child poorly if you give her a strong feeling of being loved and being respectful of others.

So much for my philosophy on how to raise happy children.

I must admit, I do miss having more time together. But it all comes with the territory, doesn't it?

I want you to know in your heart that I love you deeply.

Christopher

If Richard recalled the stories he'd heard correctly, his grandfather had died a few months before the twins were born. Richard knew his father had been very close to his own dad. The loss must have been very painful, especially at a time like that. Richard felt surprised that his dad had hardly mentioned it, listing it more as a footnote than a major life event.

Richard reasoned that it was just his father's way to keep his personal grief private. He'd seen it last week during his mother's funeral, as he had on painful occasions in the past. For the most part, his dad kept his sorrow to himself. Richard concluded that his father wanted the anniversary letter to have a positive tone. It was more an act of selflessness than a lack of acknowledgment.

It was interesting to him how different things were in the early fifties. His father had been sent to the waiting room to await the call from the doctor. With the exception of some families who couldn't afford care at that time, natural birth was unheard of. The babies were isolated at first, and the mother and baby came home after a week or so in the hospital.

His father's pride at the birth of the twins was an emotion he could readily identify with. Richard had been in the delivery room when both of his children were born. It was definitely a more intimate experience than his dad had, but the excitement was the same. Nothing could compare with that moment when months of anticipation gave way to that timeless miracle—your legacy reflected in the eyes of a newborn son or daughter.

It would be interesting to see his mother's perspective on the experience.

My dearest Christopher,

This has been such a mixed year for us, has it not? Words fall so short of conveying the joy I felt the very first moment I saw the twins. I feel so happy and proud. Ever since I was a little girl, I dreamed of having a family. You know how it goes with girls. We have a fantasy of marrying Prince Charming, having a family and making a happy home for all.

I am so fortunate to be living that fantasy this year. You are my Prince Charming, Christopher. I love you with all my heart. You are so kind and loving and thoughtful. I can already see what a wonderful father you will make.

Marie and Marcia are truly joys. They each have such different personalities. I must admit that it is a great deal of work, but it is also a labor of love and a privilege I appreciate. Thank you for being patient with me. I am sorry we don't have more time together, but that will no doubt change in about thirty years or so (ha ha).

Christopher, I am so sorry about losing Papa this year. You know how much I love him and your mother. They have always been so good to me, made me feel like a family member right from the start.

I know how close you were to him. I also know that you've kept much of your sorrow to yourself.

Yes, I know that about you, Christopher. Your sadness is very private and I will respect that. Just know that you can come to me at any time to talk about it, to cry about it, to do whatever you need to do. I love you and want to be there for you.

On this, our third anniversary together, I want you to know in your mind, your heart and your soul that I love you more with each passing day.

Yours forever,
Sarah

Richard felt a measure of sadness as he read his mother's letter. She sounded so proud, so content. Happily married and the mother of twin girls. It was forty-six years ago and she was at perhaps the height of her life.

No one but the individual can know what the height of his or her life is. That is a deeply personal conclusion, usually arrived at upon quiet reflection on one's life. An individual rarely knows it at the time. Perhaps his mother had been one of those people who knew it while it was happening. Maybe it helped her savor each moment with the understanding that the time would never come again. It wasn't a cliché to say that life moved on so very quickly.

How many times had he and Laura told each other that they should cherish the children's younger years? They both knew those years would come and go before either of them realized it. One day you're up at 2:00 A.M. changing diapers, and the next it seems you're watching them pack for college—that is, if you survived the adolescent years.

Thinking about his own girls triggered the memory of an experience he hadn't thought of for quite some time. It was one of those events that seemed so matter-of-fact on the surface but turned out to be so meaningful.

He remembered how Laura had asked him to disassemble their younger daughter's crib. Sandi had grown too old for it and they needed to make room for her new bed. Richard had been busy taking it down when he noticed a tear rolling down Laura's cheek.

He put his tools down and held her close in a moment of silent recognition. They both knew it was a time that would never come again. The girls were already growing up.

It had been a tender moment, and a part of Richard wished he could go back there now.

Fifth Anniversary

 turn of the page and every-
thing changed.

Dear Sarah,

This, our fifth anniversary, fills me with very
mixed feelings. We've had a few joyous moments
together but too many difficult ones, I'm afraid.

The birth of Peter was truly a miraculous
moment, but as the year went on, I could not help
feeling further pushed aside. Your energies were
again diverted elsewhere. Strange, isn't it, that a
father can feel jealousy toward his own children?
Sometimes I long for the earlier years before we
had them.

I want you to know that I respect you greatly as a mother. That hasn't changed. Our children are well cared for and will grow up with a healthy respect for the welfare of others, without compromising their own sense of self. We are doing fine as parents. I wish I could say the same about our marriage.

A few short years ago, you desperately wanted me, needed me. I can remember so clearly the softness of your skin as I brushed my hand across your face. You never hesitated. Now we barely make love, and it seems you do so out of marital obligation.

What a strange thing, to complain about you in this, my anniversary letter to you. Yet, I want these letters to honestly express my true feelings. In many ways, this has been an unhappy year for me.

You seem to have forgotten me. I miss the time we spent alone at night talking into the early morning hours. We would talk about everything. Love, life, family and other seemingly less significant matters, like how to grow tomatoes and whether we should splurge and buy a new radio. It didn't matter what we talked about.

I just savored every minute of watching you as you told me your thoughts and feelings. We were so close. I was mesmerized by you. Where has all of that gone lately?

My intellect understands that the children come first, but my emotions tell me I'm not getting what I need.

I love you deeply, Sarah, and in my heart I know you love me. I realize that having a family means our patience will be tested. But I don't accept that we should neglect each other's needs.

I'm sorry but I have little energy this year to write any further.

Remember though, as always, I love you.

Happy anniversary,
Christopher

Richard paused before reading his mother's response. Were these the words of his father? He'd always thought he and his father came from different worlds, but the words he had just read could easily have been his own. His father felt this neglected, too? It occurred to him that the struggles of parenthood and marriage over the generations might not be that dissimilar after all.

My dearest Christopher,

I also work hard for the family. I give my heart and soul, every hour of every day. Do you really find it so hard to accept that after taking care of our children I have little left over for you?

Christopher, our marriage is about far more than making love, and yes, I also miss it. I almost resent that you have the time to think about all your complaints. You

are a wonderful provider, but working in the house is a
special challenge, and, yes, at times I dare say a burden.

I have a secret, Christopher, one I would tell no one.
An Irish-Catholic mother of three doesn't dare think these
thoughts, let alone write them down.

Sometimes I wish I could run away, be free again, run
along the shore and feel the ocean spray on my face, drink
in a pub to my heart's content and dance in the moonlight
with a handsome foreigner who whispers in my ear that he
must have me, and do all this without guilt in my heart or
a stain upon my soul.

These thoughts appear in the strangest of places, and at
the most peculiar times.

Still, the fantasy helps me get through the day when
I am dead tired. And yes, Christopher, I long for
our earlier years together also. You were so sweet and
romantic. So caring and attentive.

Now, I sense a lack of closeness in our lovemaking.
It has become little more than mechanical for both of us.
I feel your passion has been lost in a sea of responsibility,
as has mine. Does this mean we love each other any less?

I choose to believe that these are the hard years. That
they will get better as the children get older. I always try
to remember that as difficult as these times may be, we will
both look back fondly at our children growing up. They
are all so special.

The twins with their outgoing personalities—everyone loves them. Peter—so carefree and full of life.

We must never forget we have much to be grateful for. As hard as it is, it's worth it.

Yours forever,
Sarah

There it was. The problem was time. There just wasn't enough of it. His parents' marriage had suffered neglect from a lack of time and energy. They both admitted to that.

His mother's words surprised him a little. Richard couldn't think of his own mother flirting in a pub in search of a romantic, in fact lustful, encounter—even if it was only a fantasy.

Richard and Laura had the same problem raising their daughters. It just seemed that they had less time for one another than his family had when he was growing up. Perhaps he was distorting some of his memories, but he fondly remembered family time together. No matter what they were all doing during the day, at least they'd get together for dinner. And it wasn't take-out either. His mother prepared wonderful, home-cooked, meat-and-potatoes meals. Often, she would have a homemade cake or apple crisp ready for dessert.

Every night, the entire family would sit down and carry on a communication free-for-all that seemed, at first glance, to lack particular purpose. Looking at it more carefully, Richard realized that dinner had less to do with food and more to do with bonding. As an adolescent, he often wished that his brother Peter could have been there to share his views.

Richard couldn't remember a single topic of discussion from those dinnertimes other than a lively debate about the validity of fighting Communists in Vietnam. That was back in 1968, and the events of that era left no one untouched. The family was split into two camps, and the "discussions" could become pretty heated.

The TV newscast playing in the background was going through its nightly ritual of reporting the week's body counts. Marcia started the argument.

"I think the war is immoral." She made the statement without looking their dad in the eye, knowing a reaction was coming soon enough. She didn't have long to wait.

"What do you mean 'immoral'?" He shook his head back and forth slowly for emphasis. "You don't know anything about war and oppression. That was the mistake we made back in 1939. We thought the internal struggles in Germany were a private, domestic matter. It was just a ploy that disguised the fact that the Germans wanted to dominate the world, just like the Communists."

Marie's turn came next.

"I agree with Marcia, Dad. These are different times. It's a war of independence. Just like when we wanted our separation from England during the Revolutionary War."

Their father got worked up. His voice rose and he put his fork and knife down on the plate. "You don't understand. The Communists want to take over the world."

Richard came to his father's defense. "You either stop them in Vietnam or you stop them in L.A. Besides, it's the men who fight the war."

A challenge came from left field.

Suzanne put it on the line. "Look, Dad, if you believe in the war so much, then why did you say last week you'd send Richard to Canada if he was going to be drafted?"

It was a pointed question that juxtaposed political idealism with the fact that his parents didn't want to put their son in harm's way, even though he wasn't old enough to be drafted.

Richard remembered nothing else of the conversation except that a few moments of silence passed that had seemed like hours. The details didn't matter anyway. His father would have had the final word.

He grew up in a traditional family in many ways. His parents believed in being strict. You couldn't win a power struggle with Dad or Mom. If you disagreed, you kept it to yourself and, above all, you showed no disrespect.

When they were still together, Richard and Laura probably had dinner with the children one night a week, if they were lucky. They all had different schedules and the family settled for less time together, just like other families. They grabbed meals on the run between carpooling, homework duty and late nights at the office.

Richard saw it this way: Who had any time? His philosophy was neatly articulated in a lecture he'd given a few years ago at a local university. He had titled it "Relationships Can't Be Microwaved." It was open to the public, and a mixed audience of professionals, students and others had attended.

"Life is continually being compressed into sound bites. Complicated stories are converted into a few seconds of easily digestible material. If information can be passed on in bites, why can't our relationships?"

Richard had even used himself and Laura as an example. "My wife and I fall into this trap at times ourselves. We follow along with our contemporaries and give it a catchy phrase like 'quality time.' We tell ourselves that one or two hours of focused time is better than eight hours in proximity of each other." Richard then dropped his voice, forcing the listeners to strain a little to hear what he said, with all sincerity.

"But we all know the inner secret, don't we? Deep inside ourselves we know that this concept of emotional downsizing isn't meeting anyone's needs. We are all just getting used to having less and less. Needs are being met vicariously through the experience of others.

"Movies and television are playing their parts. Why interact with our own family, which, is causing stress in the first place, when we can easily watch a sitcom where the characters seem to be having fun all the time?

"And our children, as adaptable as they are, seem to take it all in stride. Becoming a latchkey child is the norm for many of our children."

Richard had the complete attention of the audience. It was the kind of attention you receive when others know you are speaking the truth.

"And if things aren't complicated enough, many families can't afford after-school care or to have a parent stay at home. Other families are characterized by a single parent who can't possibly be at work and at home at the same time.

"It is a property of physics that a body cannot possibly be in two places at once.

"I see it in my own family. My wife, Laura, and I have the financial means to have high-quality child care. But as the children get older and don't need the constant supervision, it also gets a lot more complicated. Let me give you a recent example from our lives.

"Our older daughter, Christa, woke up one morning last week with a stomachache. Both Laura and I had very full schedules that day.

"You can't factor an unpredictable childhood sick day into a hectic day of patients and meetings. My wife and I both looked at each other and felt some relief as Christa said, 'Okay, I'll go' in response to the question, 'Are you *sure* you don't feel well enough to go to school?'

"Of course, our child was in reality trying hard to please us. I can't speak for Laura, but my guilt didn't last too long as the demands of the day took over."

Richard glanced down at the front row where Laura sat nodding her head in agreement. He thought for a moment, "Well, at least we see that the same way."

He continued with his observations. "No one factor can explain it all. Cultural evolution is simply too complicated to identify a single scapegoat we can pin it all on. It is easy to say that we simply need to get back to basic family values. But the reality is that the solutions aren't that easy, either. Society cannot go back to a time when things were less complicated.

"As far as divorce is concerned, many are the result of the complexities of modern life. And there is another factor to consider. The hectic pace most of us are caught up in flies directly in the face of basic human needs. Where does a couple find the time and energy to be intimate? And you cannot be intimate without nurturing the relationship. It's like expecting a plant to produce fruit when it hasn't been watered in years.

"It is an insidious process, this movement from lovers and friends to strangers and adversaries.

"The problem is intensified by the fact that we humans are so adaptable, we can habituate to nearly anything. That's how we can get through even the most horrific of experiences. Our survival depends on it.

"But there's a hitch. Sooner or later, basic human needs begin to assert themselves. Basic human needs are not met through microwavable solutions.

"I wish I had the answers, but at least it helps to know which questions to ask. Thank you and good night."

Judging from the applause he received, he knew he had struck a chord.

Richard thought his understanding of the issues was pretty insightful. The problem was that it hadn't helped him save his relationship with Laura. Understanding the issues was important, but it wasn't enough to keep them together. Something else was missing.

$\mathcal{S}$eventh $\mathcal{Y}$ear

$\mathcal{R}$ichard knew that the next two years of marriage would continue to be very hectic ones for his parents. During the seventh year, his sister Suzanne had been born, and he himself followed in year eight. If the last two anniversary letters were any indication, life would be getting harder, not easier.

With four children to care for, all under the age of five, things had to be more than a little nuts, Richard mused to himself for a moment. Maybe he could coin a new politically correct buzzword to describe it: *parentally challenged.*

Dear Sarah,

It's been another crazy year, hasn't it? Four children born to us in the past four years. There's no breathing time.

The children are so wonderful. Energetic and full of life. I'm exhausted but grateful. I'm trying not to complain as I have in the past. It's certainly not your fault that we have hardly any time together; it's just so frustrating at times.

You're doing a wonderful job with the children. Suzanne is a handful, isn't she? I hope the colic subsides shortly so the house is a little more peaceful. A quiet house with four children all under the age of five? How's that for a fantasy?

The pressure of making a living bothers me at times. A man's responsibility is to support his family and I accept that. You know how hard I work. I just get scared sometimes with all the bills, but somehow we'll make it. You've done a great job with the budget.

I know there hasn't been much romance in our lives lately, but I have something special for you this year, Sarah. Follow these instructions, all right?

Go out right now to the backyard.

You'll find something planted right between the two oak trees. Then come back and finish reading this letter.

Do it now! Don't read the rest of this letter until you do that.

As if it were planned, the first page ended with these words. His mother would have to follow the instructions and turn to page two. Richard felt some anticipation himself as he wondered what his father had been up to.

Surprise!!!

Do you know what it is? It's a magnolia tree I planted for you. It's a symbol of our marriage. As you may know, it's a hardy tree but one that requires care.

For it to survive and flourish, we'll have to keep an eye on it. Yet once it grows to a certain point, it will mature and require less work. Then, we can simply appreciate it more.

When you look at it over the years, know that the roots are going to continue to go deeper, and along with that the blossoms will become more pronounced. In a strong wind, the branches will bend but they won't break. If one or two do happen to break off over the years, it won't really matter as there will be many other branches and blossoms to make up for whatever beauty is lost.

I promise you, Sarah, our marriage and your new tree will continue to grow together over the years.

Love always,
Christopher

So much for the predictability of these letters. *Nice going, Dad!* Richard thought as he smiled at the romantic gesture. Now he knew where that magnolia tree came from. He never gave it any thought as a child. As far as he was concerned, it was just another tree. Now he could also understand why his parents never let any of the kids play too near it. The oaks were okay but the magnolia was off limits.

Richard remembered once that his dad had come outside and caught him and Peter hanging off the branches.

"I told you kids never to climb that tree. What the hell do you think you're doing?" He was screaming at the top of his lungs and the boys were caught completely off guard. His dad raised his voice now and again, but he never screamed.

His father had raced over to the tree and pulled them both forcibly down before they'd had a chance to respond. "Go to your room, and if I ever catch you doing that again, you'll be sorry." His dad had managed to give them each a swat on their behinds as they ran for the house.

Richard remembered his father being nicer to them later in the day. He never apologized, though; it wasn't his way. One thing was for sure: Richard and Peter never climbed that tree again.

He wasn't about to guess what his mother would write next.

Dear Christopher,

You know me. I'm going to get straight to the point. I have no life. No time to myself. This is no "lucky seven" year for me. I feel like I'm drowning in an endless sea of responsibility. Cooking, cleaning, bathing, washing clothes, changing diapers, cleaning up vomit, taking

temperatures, making sure the children are bundled up
when we go out in the cold.

Here's an example of my insane life these days. Try
taking four children to the supermarket during a snow-
storm. One has a cold, another has diarrhea and the other
two are fighting constantly. Then when we get back home,
I get to wash all our clothes by hand. That's twenty-seven
shirts and pants, ninety-two diapers, thirty-seven pairs of
underwear.

Did I mention forty-two towels and five sets of sheets?
Who's counting? After that I get to prepare dinner, and
let's not forget I iron your clothes for the next day.

Meanwhile, the twins and Peter are into everything
and require a constant watchful eye.

This isn't much of an anniversary letter, is it?

I love you and the children. You know that.

It just gets overwhelming sometimes. I wish my mother
lived closer. She'd be such a help. You work so many hours,
Christopher. I know you're doing your best also. It's a lot
of responsibility to earn the income to support the family.

I sense your resentment at times, though. You want me
as a woman, not just as a mother. Don't you think I
know that? It's reasonable but unrealistic.

You want me to greet you at the door after a sixteen-
hour day in a robe that has a sexy negligee hidden

underneath and say to you, "I want you now!" But
we both know the reality. It's what we signed on for.

It's not that I'm mad at you, Christopher. I understand
what you need. We both need it, but we're in the same boat.

The children come first. That's just the way it is. You
don't really think we're in a unique position, do you? It's
really nature. Men and women meet. They're attracted.
Have sex. Have babies and devote many years to raising
them. Nothing you or I say or feel will change that.
But all in all, that's okay. Because the children do give
us so much pleasure as well. Bringing children into the
world is a gift and a privilege.

It helps me to keep in mind something my grandmother
always told me. "They will grow up overnight. You'll
wake up one morning and they'll be on their own."

They're young now and need us. And believe this:
Someday we will wish for these days again.

Let's continue to appreciate this great gift. And you
know what, Christopher? It's all right to complain about
how hard it is at the same time that we are grateful.
There's no contradiction in this as far as I am concerned.

Judging from the beginning of this letter, you might
think I'm a little bit crazy this year. Well, the truth is, I
am a little. My emotions go up and down, and I appreciate your being patient with me.

Oh, and, there is something else Christopher. I still look at you and see the handsome, vibrant man I fell in love with.

Every morning I still put on some makeup to remind me of my femininity and kiss you on your way out the door to remind you that I'm your woman. The best parts of our relationship might be on hold most of the time, but they are not forgotten.

Forgive this somewhat rambling and disjointed letter. It's a reflection of my life these days.

Happy anniversary, sweetheart.

Love,
Sarah

His mother hadn't mentioned the magnolia tree. Surely she would have if she had known about it. Richard concluded that his mother had written these anniversary letters before or at the same time his father had. Maybe it was her way of expressing herself without the influence of what he had written.

Richard always felt some guilt because sometimes he privately thought that having children was a major sacrifice. Now he knew his parents had felt the same way.

Richard thought back to when he was a child sitting on the living room floor watching shows like *Father Knows Best*, *Leave It to Beaver*, *Ozzie and Harriet*, and *The Donna Reed Show*. He'd observe the antics of each episode and absorb the unconscious message that they all had great marriages and loved being parents.

A couple of months ago, he admitted it in a session with Dr. Allison: "I don't love being a parent all the time. I love my daughters but not the responsibility that goes along with raising them."

"That's pretty normal, Richard."

"Not according to the way I was raised. My parents loved being parents all the time."

Richard had always held onto that belief, until this last letter.

Still, it was confusing to try to understand what had gone on during his parents' generation. Richard wondered about it. *Did parents then really enjoy it all more, or did they just get caught up in their roles and what was expected of them? When you're programmed carefully, you don't question very much. On the other hand, maybe today's relationships are in more trouble because they conflict with the prime directive of raising a family.*

He reflected that he would never even remotely have guessed that his parents struggled with being parents, especially not his mother. But here it was in her own handwriting—she struggled with the demands of parenthood. She was human too.

Richard realized that life was more complicated now than it had been during previous generations. His parents' generation and those before it simply married and had babies. Couples didn't make a lifestyle choice about whether to have a family or how many children to have. They just did it. Nowadays, becoming a parent was a choice. Many couples elected to remain childless, while others who were incapable of having children adopted or sought medical intervention that could make having their own children possible. Others delayed parenthood until their late thirties or early forties, after they had established careers, traveled and enjoyed couplehood.

In his practice, Richard had seen several couples who dealt with the question of whether or not to have children. He saw that question as one that could arise only in a culture where people chose their way of life. Of course, he also saw in his work that too many choices could overwhelm and confuse people.

There was something else apparent in these words he was reading. His parents, in many ways, had it a lot tougher than he and Laura did. They had very few conveniences. He'd just read how washing clothes had been a major production. And yet, when he looked at photos taken during his childhood, it was clear how clean and polished they all looked.

Richard thought about one photograph in particular that his sister Suzanne had hanging in her living room. Whenever he came to visit her, he studied it carefully. It was a picture of all the children, including Peter, that had been taken when Richard was four years old.

During the spring and summer, the family would go to a nearby lake every Sunday after church and feed bread to the swans that gathered there. His mom would always take some leftover bread and give each of the children a slice or two. They would listen to the swans squawk and fight to get a piece. Richard remembered that no matter how much bread they brought along, it never seemed to be enough to satisfy either the swans or the children.

Peter was standing next to him in the photograph. Both of the boys had on freshly ironed, dark suits with crisp, white shirts and clip-on ties. Marie and Marcia were dressed in pristine, matching white dresses, along with white gloves. Suzanne stood between them. She had on a dress that Richard's mother had once remarked was dark peach with a pair of blue bows on each shoulder, though the black and white photo prevented him from verifying this fact. All five children's hair was neatly combed and groomed. The polished toes of their shoes reflected the sun. The picture didn't lie— it showed his parents' total devotion and self-sacrifice.

Richard and Laura had a lawn service, a pool service, a handyman and a baby-sitter, as well as a housekeeper who came twice a week.

How pathetic, he thought. The vast majority of people didn't have these luxuries to make life easier.

Still, he knew it wasn't as though their professional lives were without pressure. In fact, sometimes he believed *that* was the cause. He and Laura had too many outside demands and responsibilities. Perhaps having the lawn to mow wasn't so much the problem as treating one too many patients or having to prepare for a big trial.

In any case, Richard now saw that his parents were more sophisticated in their understanding of what marriage was all about than he had previously acknowledged. He found that rather impressive considering that, at this point in time in the anniversary letters, they still had forty-two years of marriage ahead of them. Richard was interested to see what insights and perhaps secrets the remaining letters held.

The letters had brought his parents to life. They appeared as they had been when they wrote the letters. Though written far in the past, they created anticipation about the future.

Eighth Anniversary

ichard was born in the eighth year of his parents' marriage. He surmised that his father had probably included this anniversary because of that. Their marital narrative would finally include references to him. He knew, coming so soon after the birth of Suzanne, that his parents must have felt exhausted.

By this time his dad was twenty-nine and his mother twenty-eight. They were no doubt veterans at this pregnancy and childbirth routine. Having five children by the time you were in your late twenties was remarkable by today's standards. Richard and Laura had their firstborn at around the same ages. It was a little hard to imagine how different things had been then.

He was now reading about himself as the newest member of the family. It seemed as though he were reading a play and a new character was entering the scene for the first time. But this was no play he was reading. It was his own life and heritage—it was real. He wondered what his parents would say about him.

Dear Sarah,

Where did last year go? I feel as though I just penned the last anniversary letter a moment ago. The children do make time go so fast. I didn't expect them to be growing quite so quickly. You must be giving them an extra watering without my knowledge.

Marie and Marcia do have quite a vocabulary going. And this twin phenomenon is very interesting to watch. They have different personalities, yet they're so in touch with what the other is thinking and feeling.

Don't they look adorable on Sundays when they're dressed up in the same outfits for church?

Suzanne reminds me so much of you. She's so loving and giving—always willing to share.

And I must tell you that I feel so much pride in my heart when Peter and I go outside and toss a ball.

With all the pressures, I feel I'm adjusting pretty well to our crazy-paced life. It's a question of developing a routine and just getting used to things. I must say that experience helps.

I also feel as though you and I have done a better job of making the routine less of a rut. The fights we had were very intense at times and upset both of us. Had we not been married, we might have broken up over them. I think we both know that.

In a way, perhaps they were helpful arguments because I believe we now understand each other better.

Getting out together alone once a week to a movie or dinner has helped a lot. I look forward to our "date." It doesn't take a genius to figure out that we have to take some time out just for ourselves if we want our relationship to have any identity of its own.

Remember how your father and mother would go behind the house and pick vegetables by themselves once a week? It was just for a few minutes, but they wouldn't let any of the kids be involved. You thought they were being mean until you realized when you got older that it was their special time together, even if it was just for a few minutes a week.

Well, now Richard's going to keep that cycle of late-night feedings up for a while, isn't he? That's fine. He's an absolute joy. I think he looks like you. Same eyes and smile.

When I first saw you holding him, I felt this overwhelming sense of happiness and pride. It happens the same way each time we have a baby. I wasn't sure how we'd both feel about another child so close on the heels of Suzanne. But there's nothing routine about this miracle and blessing. Each time I prepare myself for the birth as best as a father can. My experience is always different from yours. After all, you're the one carrying our child and giving birth.

We know the drill: contractions properly spaced, then off to the hospital. If it's not a false alarm, next comes the waiting—then the wondering and the worrying. Finally the doctor brings the news. I thank God that the baby and you are healthy, and my heart sings with joy when I see our child for the first time.

Sarah, please never tire of these words: I love you with all my heart. You're a wonderful wife and mother. I believe that we've succeeded in adjusting to this time in our lives during the past few years.

I always miss spending more time alone together, but as long as we remain healthy there'll be time for us again later.

The magnolia tree is coming along well, isn't it?

Love,
Christopher

Since the last set of anniversary letters, his dad sounded calmer. Richard would have expected his birth to have caused even more stress, but the tone of the letter was definitely different this year. Richard wondered about what had happened during that time. He expected that things were still tough.

In some ways, Richard felt as though he might be missing out on some important events in their lives. He couldn't even say why; it was just a sense he had. But he respected the fact that his dad had every right to reveal or hold back whatever he pleased. That was the deal.

But that didn't change the frustration of wanting to know how his father had made the transition into what looked like the traditional family man. On the other hand, Richard knew that family men were more common in earlier generations than nowadays.

His father's letter was clearly one of acceptance. But Richard wanted to know more. It's easy to say "I accept this or I accept that" in a marriage, but working it into the daily fabric of your married life was altogether different. The simple letters didn't reveal all he wanted to know.

He was curious about those fights his father mentioned. They must have been intense if his father thought the fights could have broken them up under different circumstances. He could hardly remember any squabbles between his parents, let alone any fights, while he was growing up. Richard guessed that they must have worked out the major kinks in their marriage before he was born. Either then, or while he was too young to remember.

He'd love to ask his father sometime. Maybe he would if his dad ever gave him permission to ask questions about the letters. Richard already resolved, out of respect, never to ask anything unless invited to do so. By now he only had about a thousand or so questions.

It was also apparent to Richard that by this anniversary his father seemed to be reaching some level of balance in his life. He was finding room in his life to be both a father and a husband. His father also seemed more philosophical about the daily stresses he and his wife faced.

Richard knew this to be true because the letters were honest. It was apparent that when things were good the letters were upbeat, and when things were bad they weren't. These letters clearly reflected the truth. They were real.

Changes had also taken place for his mother during the past few years of the marriage. That was a guarantee. The entry he had just read a minute ago sounded as though she was pretty overwhelmed. That could only have become worse, not better. Richard wondered if she, too, had managed to preserve her philosophy of family and marriage. In the face of the reality of her life as she was living it in the trenches, that would be a challenge.

Dear Christopher,

Happy anniversary! What a year it's been. Richard is precious, isn't he? And the other children are so excited to have a new brother. I think Peter is pleased that he's less outnumbered by his sisters.

All the children are doing well and we can feel grateful for that. They are being well cared for and loved. It certainly is a lot of work, though. Between your demands at the office and mine at home, we hardly have time to take a breath. Still, I think sometimes to myself how much better it is to have a life with meaning. I may feel overwhelmed with being a mother much of the time, but I do enjoy it more than I did in earlier years.

As the children are getting a little older, it is getting somewhat easier. And watching their personalities develop is so much fun. I feel sorry that you miss much of this because you are away at work.

You know something, Christopher? Much of our lives revolve around raising our children, but I've discovered that what's important to me goes beyond that. My relationships with others are a basic joy, especially with other adults. A mother can easily forget how to communicate with other adults when she spends so much time around young ones.

My friendship with Mary has deepened, and it's a great relief to have a neighbor to spend a few moments with. We enjoy our morning coffee even with the children running around us. I find a measure of peace in those few moments.

We talk about all sorts of things, from the children, of course, to how we feel about life and our marriages. It helps me through the day.

I am pleased with how we are doing as a couple. I think we've settled nicely into a family life together. Our relationship isn't perfect, but it doesn't need to be. We have each other's well-being in mind, and that's what matters most.

Anniversaries are markers, aren't they? A day to take time and reflect on the day we were married.

I think of our wedding day in detail every year and look at our album. It was a wonderful day. I look at my mother in our pictures together and do feel sadness that she *isn't here, but I don't belabor it.*

We can be proud in this, our eighth year together, that we've done as well as we have.

I love you, Christopher, and am grateful and happy that you are in my life.

Sarah

Richard's first reaction was relief that his parents were definitely on the same page. That was comforting. He was happy to see that he himself was born at a time when they seemed happy. Even reading this as an adult, he would have felt some discomfort if he'd been born during a rough time. He wouldn't have been able to help feeling he was an additional burden.

Richard could also see that his father and mother were acting more and more like a team. They were realizing that they were working toward the same goal. With that realization came the awareness that their own needs would have to continue to take a back seat. Instead of fighting that fact, they were accepting it.

Richard had forgotten about his mother's friend, Mary, until the letter reminded him. He was, of course, oblivious to any relationship his mother and Mary might have had. He vaguely remembered going next door in the mornings to play sometimes. Having a supportive friend had clearly made a difference to his mom. Thinking back, he was sure that she missed Mary when his father's company transferred them to San Francisco in early 1964.

Reading about his mother's friend made him think about Laura. It was one of her problems, he believed. She really didn't have any close friends she could share her feelings with. Richard thought it contributed to their problems.

He knew that her own family life had been hard. Laura was an only child, and her mother had died when she was only ten years old. She and her father had a falling out—eight years ago, over his new wife—and they hadn't talked since then. Richard often felt bad for Laura, knowing her father lived only five miles away. Sometimes, Richard would ask her if she wanted him to try to make contact with her father on her behalf. Laura's response was always an unequivocal no.

She had been deeply hurt and had learned to protect herself. Unfortunately, Richard knew that although her protective wall kept others out, it trapped Laura inside herself at times.

"You need to find a friend to talk to, Laura. You're too locked up inside," he would tell her. Sometimes he meant it to be a caring statement, and other times it he meant for it to provoke her. It didn't really matter how he had intended it—Laura always responded the same way.

"I don't need to talk to anybody about my personal life. I can handle things on my own." It frustrated Richard to no end to hear her say this.

"Maybe you'll feel better if you have a place to vent your frustrations."

"Sounds like psychobabble to me, Richard. No one can help solve our problems but you and I." Richard agreed with that to a point, but they rarely could have a productive discussion without it becoming an argument. That had been especially true during the past year or so.

Richard looked out the window and admired the clouds as he flew high above the earth. He was pleased to know that his parents were as sophisticated as he had discovered. He'd been believing a myth all these years. It was the myth that parents and people in general had been simpler in earlier generations.

It was a belief that he had carefully kept preserved in his mind, like a delicate piece of china. He had thought about it at times over the years when life's complexities overwhelmed him. At those exasperating moments, he might have said to himself, "At least Dad and Mom had an uncomplicated life full of fulfillment and joy."

Things were different now. Reading the letters had shattered that particular piece of emotional china, and along with it his childhood myths, forever. Their values may have been straightforward and simple, but they were far from being uncomplicated people.

Year Fifteen

*R*ichard wished he could just skip the next exchange of anniversary letters. He didn't need to start reading to know what had happened that year.

On August third at around four o'clock in the afternoon, Richard's life and the lives of the rest of his family changed forever.

Richard recalled that it was a hot day. He cooled himself under the lawn sprinkler with Suzanne, while Peter went down to the river to swim with his friends. They swam every day, and Richard was frustrated that he was too young to go along.

Sometime later, Peter's best friend Eric came running up to the house screaming hysterically. Richard's mother came out and tried to calm him down so she could understand what he was saying.

"It's Peter. I think he's dead! I think he's dead!" Richard remembered that Eric must have said that a hundred times.

"I think he's dead," rolled over and over in Richard's seven-year-old mind, but he couldn't understand it. He remembered thinking that if this was one of their tricks, they'd be in big trouble when Dad came home.

But that had been Richard's wishful thinking. As soon as he had looked at Eric's terrified face and into his glazed eyes, he knew this was no trick.

Richard had started to run toward the river, but his mother caught him and demanded he stay put with his sisters. He remembered her running off with Eric. She screamed over her shoulder for one of the twins to call an ambulance.

The rest of the day was mostly a blur. The only other detail he could remember was finding out that an undertow had swept Peter under a pile of logs and he had drowned. Eric had tried desperately to free him.

Richard had struggled to accept what had happened. Peter and he had just had a fight that very morning, and they would have made up and played together again that night, just like always.

Mortality wasn't something Richard seriously considered at the age of seven. When he and Peter played army and shot each other, they couldn't even lie dead for more than a minute or two. No one in his family was supposed to die. They were supposed to have fun and live as though life went on forever.

Even when he saw the ambulance screaming by his house, he thought it was exciting, and that he and Peter would talk about it all when he came home.

Richard waited up that night, looking out the window and waiting. He didn't believe his mother when she said that Peter had gone to heaven. He had decided that although she'd never been wrong about anything before, she was definitely wrong about this.

In the days that followed, he saw that maybe it was true. Maybe Peter wasn't coming home after all. Richard remembered crying himself to sleep one night as he looked out his window above the front porch. He had hoped to see his brother appear from the shadows and walk into the glow cast by the streetlight outside their house. But he never appeared.

Richard recalled his mother crying for what seemed like hours at a time after Peter's death. She had been hysterical at first. As soon as his father came home, she had calmed down a little. He remembered that. He also recalled thinking that his dad would fix it all—straighten out this mess, bring Peter home and calm down his mom.

But Richard knew that Peter was really dead when Father O'Malley came to the house to visit. He had always shaken his hand after Mass, but he'd never imagined Father would ever come to their house. Priests were bigger than life. They were mysterious and scary beings who sat in the darkness of a confessional box where, when you were old enough, you told them all your deepest and darkest secrets. You told them things you would tell no one else except perhaps your best friend . . . or your brother.

Richard remembered the exact moment he realized Peter was dead.

He had peeked around the corner into the living room and had seen Father O'Malley whispering quietly to his father and mother. Then with a simple sign of the cross, he had blessed them both. It was a blessing that came straight from God, and it was reserved for special cases.

Special cases like death.

Richard hadn't gone to his brother's funeral. It was his parents' way. They hadn't wanted him to have any more sad memories than necessary.

Other things had changed too. Mom didn't comb his hair quite so carefully every morning, and once she even let Suzanne go to church in a dress that had a stain on it.

It didn't surprise Richard to see that his father's letter wasn't more than a paragraph.

Dear Sarah,

I'm trying so hard to make sense of what happened. I know I should have faith, but I can't find it. I love all the children and am grateful for them, but there is a hole inside me that will never fully heal. I know you feel the same. We have to pull together for the sake of the children and our own sanity.

I love you and will be there for you.

Love,
Christopher

It was an unintentional lie. Dad had slipped into a depression that year. Richard knew that because his uncle had told him. His father couldn't possibly have been there for his mother. He had nothing to give and was making promises he wasn't able to keep.

Richard picked up his mother's letter knowing she'd somehow try and make things right.

Christopher,

I'm not sure what I can say this year. I feel a combination of anger and despair. Some of it is toward you. I know that you're suffering. But this isn't a time to pull away, is it? It's a time when I need you more than ever. We need each other more than ever.

All I want you to do is hold me tight and tell me everything is going to be all right. I want you to tell me that, even though I know it can never possibly be true. Don't you understand that?

I desperately need the belief and the hope that we will make it through as a family. Can't you even do that for me? I'm tired of being strong. I'm tired of crying myself quietly to sleep at night because I don't trust you with my feelings. Don't run away from me, Christopher.

I must be there for the children. They need a mother

who's strong now. I can do my best to fake it with them. But I don't want to fake it with you. I need you to be there for me.

Get out of your shell and let's help each other.

This tragedy didn't happen to you or to me. It happened to us.

I love you,
Sarah

Richard knew that it wasn't unusual to see a tragedy pull a couple apart. But these were his parents, not just any couple. He thought for sure that his mother would have responded with compassion to her husband's grief. But of course, she was suffering, too.

Richard realized that it was a good thing his father hadn't seen that letter at the time it was written. It would only have served to make him feel more guilty. Richard wondered what his father had felt when he read these words recently. Had the guilt stretched out over thirty-four years and found its mark again? Or had his father put it all in perspective?

Despite her intentions otherwise, Richard thought that his mother must have communicated her anger somehow. It wasn't the kind of emotion anyone could keep under wraps indefinitely. He guessed that she must have screamed at him in a fit of uncontrollable grief and rage. That must have been quite a fight.

Year fifteen had to have been the lowest point in their marriage. It couldn't get any worse than this: the loss of a child and, with it, a piece of their hearts. And to top it off, an inability to take care of each other.

They must have felt so desperately alone.

In a way, Richard felt a sense of shame. He and Laura had their difficult times, but nothing that compared to this.

Eighteenth Anniversary

Reading about his brother's death caused Richard to think about Laura's point of view again. Like most people, when he experienced deep emotional losses he found that his own pre-occupations suddenly seemed less significant.

It really wasn't something he wanted to rethink. They were going to be divorced, and it was no time for him to feel empathic toward the opposition. He had been through all that.

He recalled one of the many marital therapy sessions they'd gone through about a year ago. He had listened to her in the same way that some of his own patients listen to each other when forced to do so in the controlled environment of a counselor's office.

Their therapist, Dr. Angela Thompson, was very skilled. She knew just how to balance the sessions in such a way that both parties felt their points of view were understood. She was also practical in her approach and gave them assignments to work on between sessions. He recalled one session in particular.

"Richard," Dr. Thompson had begun in her soft, measured voice with its faint Southern accent. "I don't think you're really listening to what Laura is saying to you." She had turned to Laura. "Now go ahead and tell him again."

"It's not that I don't care enough about the marriage. It's just that I'm exhausted all the time. I have a busy law practice, two children and all the responsibility that goes with that. I'm sick of hearing about how neglected *you* feel. I'm not exactly living my life in Club Med these days." Her voice grew louder. He could see the anger welling inside her.

"Richard, it sounds to me like Laura's overwhelmed."

She had turned to Laura again. "Maybe there are some more things Richard can do to help. Then it will be up to you to take more time out for him." She directed the next question to both of them. "Fair enough?"

Richard had responded. "It's fair enough but too simple. I think I help a lot. We're both tired, but I still have the energy for her."

"All right, then. I suggest you take some more of that energy that you have left over for Laura and use it to help her. The way I see these things working, you'll both do better in your marriage when you decide to get off each other's backs and take better care of each other. Just a little down-home advice my mother gave me."

Dr. Thompson smiled. It was a disarming smile that revealed kindness and held an understanding of human nature, forged as a result of hearing many thousands of hours of problems that men and women experienced in their relationships.

Both Richard and Laura had gone through the motions. It had helped for a while, but before long their marriage reverted back to the way it had been, with Richard again feeling neglected.

A colleague had once referred to this as the "rubber band theory of change." You can stretch your behavior to a certain length to please your partner. Eventually, your personality causes you to snap back and be yourself. Richard wasn't interested in being a rubber band anymore.

Still, Richard had to admit to himself that he wasn't the most sensitive person in the world. It was not a simple admission.

He had always accused Laura of being cold and hard. He used to tell her during arguments that the "sensitivity gene" had somehow skipped over her. It might have been a clever insult, but it certainly hadn't helped them move forward.

On another occasion he had told her, "Trying to get you to admit anything is like trying to get through the armor on a tank with a BB gun. I can keep firing forever but I'll never get through. You're the most insensitive person I've ever known."

But Richard knew better. He knew very well that an insensitive person doesn't have layer upon layer of psychological armor. He'd seen a million times that the intensity of psychological defenses was directly proportional to what they were designed to protect. Laura was precisely as tough on the outside as she was sensitive on the inside.

This idea of Laura's armor made Richard think about his own. He concluded that now would be a good time to tighten up his own emotional defenses. There wasn't any value in understanding Laura better at this point. Their problems were way beyond that.

Dear Sarah,

I almost didn't write you this year. But I promised you a letter every anniversary, and so here it is. With the loss of Peter three years ago, I was completely devastated. You know how special he was to me. I miss him terribly. I feel an anger and a rage that cannot be directed anywhere. I don't know what to do with my sadness.

You are angry at me, I know, for not being there more to help you with your own anguish, and I am sorry for that. I also feel very bad about the pain my relationship with Claire has caused you.

I ask you now to try to get past what has happened.

My liaison with Claire was not about sex. It was about a need for attention and warmth, which I haven't gotten for such a long time.

I must tell you that I am not completely sorry about the affair. There were so many times I wanted to just run away and forget all the pain and sadness. My responsibilities to my family, my love for you and the children wouldn't allow me to run.

I do not ask for forgiveness. I only ask for some understanding. Life is very complicated. Let's try to move on.

I love you dearly, Sarah. Always have, always will.

                                        Yours,
                                        Christopher

Richard read the letter again, disbelieving the words scrawled in his father's own writing. But the words were clear. He may have wished otherwise, but this was the truth.

My father had an affair! Richard, as an adult, had considered the possibility that perhaps his father might have strayed, but he had never imagined it could be true. Now here it was, right in front of him.

Richard didn't know at first what shocked him most. Was it the fact that his father had an affair, or the fact that his dad, by sharing this letter with him, was intentionally letting him know about it.

This was no simple admission.

Richard realized that his father came from a generation that was very quiet about these matters. People didn't flaunt such things then. Fidelity, real or imagined, was an important part of the marital culture. He knew that it would have been easy enough to edit this segment of the anniversary letters, and Richard would have been none the wiser.

But it was clear to him that his father believed there was a greater purpose to be served. Sharing the reality of the struggles in his parents' marriage was more important than risking his son's judgment about him as a person. It took a special kind of courage to do that.

Richard wasn't unfamiliar with extramarital affairs. Both he and Laura were guilty of infidelity. They had told each other during an argument one night, just before they separated. Not that it was really a surprise to either of them.

He thought referring to them as affairs was a technicality, considering that Richard and Laura were seriously headed for a divorce at the time they occurred.

Still, they were hard to accept.

He knew that it wasn't easy for either him or Laura to live with the knowledge that they each had been with someone else. That was true even at the point of divorce.

It was one thing if you were beyond loving someone, but Richard knew in his heart that he and Laura still loved each other. He told himself that they had turned elsewhere out of loneliness and a need for attention.

The truth was that the affairs had made them both feel better, even though it had been a temporary fix. It was a relief to find someone who valued you again. Someone who thought you were wonderful and flawless, even if it was only a fantasy.

Richard's affair with Susan had lasted six months. He had worked with her at one of the hospitals where he was an attending psychiatrist. Susan was the hospital's admissions coordinator. She spoke with Richard about cases and saw him a few times a week. He knew her for about two years before they crossed the line.

To say that it began innocently enough would be untrue. The basic chemistry that pulls men and women together is anything but innocent. Sometimes it's just disguised so that the participants themselves are unaware of it.

And so it was with Richard when he had invited Susan for coffee at the hospital cafeteria one morning. They got to know each other more personally.

Susan had been married for twelve years and had three children of her own. She had a full-time career and was working part time on an MBA. She was attractive and bright, and had a great sense of humor. After some superficial exchanges, she learned of his unhappiness at home, and he of hers. He had come out and asked her directly.

"How are things at home? I mean married life?" It wasn't an innocuous question. Richard was probing and he knew it. Susan knew it, too.

Susan looked straight into his eyes and turned her smile into a serious expression that would not confuse the message she was about to send.

"It sucks and it's lonely."

"I'm sorry," Richard responded. That was true and untrue at the same time. He did feel sorry for her, but he was also hopeful that they might be able to get together.

The opportunity came soon enough at the hospital Christmas party. Laura wasn't able to attend. Her own office party was the same night. Neither of them cared if they went alone at that point. In fact, each was secretly relieved that they wouldn't have to fake the happy couple routine just for political purposes.

Richard and Susan had a little too much to drink and ended up in the on-call room. It was adolescent and thrilling. He remembered every detail. He took her gently by the hand and whispered in her ear, "Follow me." It was a bold move with a touch of danger and much excitement. Richard quietly closed the door behind them and locked it. They were both nervous. He had fantasized about this moment many times, but reality has a way of bringing up fear.

He turned to Susan and without saying a word gently kissed her. She responded passionately and pulled him closer. Whatever anxiety they felt initially disappeared in the naturalness of their connection.

Richard undressed her slowly. She was wearing a black

cocktail dress with thin straps that he pulled off her shoulders as he kissed her neck. Susan slowly unbuttoned his shirt and they lay down on the bed.

For the next few minutes the world around them didn't exist. It was just the two of them. A man and a woman attracted to each other—lonely and in need.

They had no thoughts of responsibilities. No children. No party going on outside. No guilt. Just a moment in time that they would both have for the rest of their lives. Their lovemaking was passionate and intense. He felt the electricity between them intensify with every kiss and every touch. They were lost in each other—two people who had felt desperately alone for far too long.

After that first encounter, they met once a week or so whenever they could arrange it. It was never again as spontaneous. It became a part of the rest of their lives. A planned affair. A relationship that fit somehow into their crazy lives. They both knew it was time limited.

Richard and Susan cared about each other but they weren't in love. It ended when they both realized it wasn't going anywhere. They still saw each other occasionally at the hospital, but it was never the same.

Richard didn't know much about Laura's affair. For all he knew, she still might be seeing Stephen. What he did know was that Stephen, whom he had met briefly some years before, was a partner in Laura's law practice. He couldn't even remember what he looked like, though he had been curious now and again. He never had pushed for details. It wasn't something he wanted to know much about. She worked with him every day and that was enough.

Then it hit him. His private reflections suddenly stopped as a thought forced its way up from his unconscious mind. Something in the last letter he read was important. It was as though his mind was reminding him to come back into the moment.

Claire was the name of Walter's wife!

Walter had been his dad's best friend, and he had died many years ago in a hunting accident. Was this the woman his dad had an affair with?

Of course, Richard thought. *Who else?* Although a part of him wanted to, he couldn't dismiss it. Just like the phone call informing him of his mother's death, this was real life.

Claire had remained friends with both his parents for years. The friendship never ended. As a matter of fact, his mother kept in touch with Claire right up to her death, and Richard saw Claire himself a couple years ago when she passed through Miami on her way to a vacation in Aruba. Claire even attended his mother's funeral.

Not surprisingly, a number of questions flooded Richard's mind at once. Why had his mother continued to have a relationship with Claire over the years? Did Claire know that his mother knew? Perhaps his mother's anniversary letter would satisfy some of his curiosity.

Christopher,

I never thought it was possible to love someone so deeply in a marriage, yet contemplate divorcing that person on a daily basis. However, this is where I find myself on this, our eighteenth, anniversary.

I was deeply hurt by your relationship with Claire. I so wanted to believe that mine was the only bed you would share for the rest of our lives. Mine the only body you would feel so close. Perhaps these were just the naive wishes of a young woman who had a fantasy of how a marriage would be. Didn't we promise each other "for better or worse"? "For richer or poorer"? Or was that my imagination?

The last few years have been the poorest in our marriage. Hard times, lean years. Yet, I always had faith that we were at a stage that we would pass through. Not unscarred perhaps, but we would get through it and find a life together again on the other side.

Everything has changed.

Our marriage is not going at all as I had hoped. When we married, Christopher, I knew that there would be hard times, but not like this. At twenty, I was in love and unprepared. My mother's advice seems to have fallen so short. I'm sure she and my father never had to deal with problems like this.

My parents handled their marriage much better than we do ours. Perhaps they had as many, or dare I say more, problems to contend with. After all, who really knows the inner workings of any relationship? One sees what is presented.

And they raised eight children, not four, without numerous advantages and conveniences. But perhaps the key is that they seem to have accepted things better. I will never know now that they are both gone. How I wish I could call upon my mother now, in this time of need, to ask her if it was the same for her.

As for the affair, Christopher, I must tell you that if I look deep inside me, I feel that I am partially to blame. I know that I had no energy for you, and certainly none for myself. I'm smart enough to know that we are both to blame. However, my anger will not allow me to openly admit this to you. I'm afraid that you will think that what you did was somehow all right. It will never be all right.

I sometimes feel badly for not sharing these letters with you over the years. They have been an escape for me . . . a way to express my deepest thoughts and feelings. You know most of them already, but this year is different. I'm glad to keep these thoughts and feelings to myself. I hate you and love you all at the same time. How can this be?

Sarah

The letter didn't begin with "Dear" this year. There was no ending of "Love" or "Yours always" either.

The questions that Richard raised about Claire looked as though they wouldn't be answered, at least not in this letter. He was having a hard time imagining that his mother had accepted the affair as well as she seemed to. It just didn't work that way in real life.

But by now Richard knew that his parents were far from conventional. His mother's realization that his father had carried on an affair out of need was a sophisticated understanding of human nature. Claire was a widow and his father a grieving man, and they were both vulnerable and lonely.

His mother's letter revealed the intellectual understanding and personal pain that accompany such sophistication. She had been quite a woman.

But of course, he knew that both his parents had felt deep pain. No one had a corner on the market. In the last three years of their letters, they had lost a son and struggled with the consequences of his father's affair. On top of that, they still had four children to care for—four children who had lost a brother.

Richard realized that this was his parents' own ground zero.

The only way to pick themselves up each morning and go on was to tap into a resource deep inside themselves. His parents were operating on pure commitment and hope.

Commitment to each other and the family. Hope that things would get better.

It was the only explanation for how they possibly could have found the inner strength to endure.

Year Twenty

Richard looked forward with anticipation to reading what had happened during year twenty. It had been five years since the death of his brother and two since the affair. His professional experience taught him that people didn't heal that quickly. Personal experience with Laura showed him that there was a part that never healed. Their affairs still hurt them even though they were separated and waiting for the final divorce decree.

But they *would* get divorced and move on. The affairs would be a part of their deteriorated history: a postscript to a dead marriage.

His parents were the ones who had the real challenge.

They somehow had moved beyond what had happened and stayed together.

Richard understood human nature. He knew that his mother would have had to find it inside herself to move on.

Her adjustment couldn't have been easy.

Nor could his father's adjustment have been easy. Whatever void Claire had filled for him, she was now gone. The void would remain, but the relief she provided would disappear.

Whatever they were, needs were needs. Would his father have found it inside himself to once again let his marriage meet his needs, or would he have learned to do without?

As far as his mother was concerned, maybe if she had become involved with someone herself, it would have helped her. It was easier to accept if you had an affair yourself. Then you could at least justify in your own mind that you'd evened the score. She, too, had her needs.

But his mother never would have had an affair, not in a million years. She just hadn't been that way. She had held very strong beliefs about marriage and commitment. Her personal challenge would have been to find a way to accept what her husband had done and move on.

Her husband. It sounded so abstract at the moment. Her husband was Richard's father. This wasn't some clinical case unfolding in front of him. It was about his father and his mother.

Richard moved his father's letter aside for the moment and read his mother's first. He couldn't wait to see what she had to say.

Dear Christopher,

Happy anniversary, Christopher. Another year has passed and I can hardly believe that this is our twentieth anniversary. We've had some rough times together (isn't that an understatement?), but all in all we've done well. I love you and want you to know that you are a wonderful husband and father.

I often reflect on what my life would have been like if I'd not met you, let alone not married you. Surely it would have been a poorer life.

The children are doing well. The twins have been feeling their oats this year, haven't they? They have become somewhat of a handful at age seventeen. They don't listen to me as well as I'd like them to. It's not as though I ask much of them; their responsibilities are light when compared with what mine were at their age.

I realize that their friends, and boys, are becoming more important than their parents. That's the natural course of events. But natural or not, I miss my little girls and feel some sadness watching them pull away from me. They don't need me quite as much, and that scares any mother who has devoted the last seventeen years of her life to raising them.

Suzanne is coming along fine, don't you think? She's

probably watching her older sisters with a sense of awe as they apply makeup, change clothes constantly and giggle about boys. I must say that there is some relief in seeing that she still enjoys playing with dolls.

Richard is an active and inquisitive child. He seems to have adjusted to the change that took place in his life a few years ago better than I would have anticipated. I must give you and Steve credit for that. He needs the male influence, considering he is surrounded by girls.

I do feel a little sad this year knowing that it is just a matter of time before the twins are finally grown. Soon they will marry their sweethearts and move out. I already know that day is coming all too soon.

One of the benefits of marriage, though, is the fact that we'll have each other, Christopher. Strange, isn't it? We started off together just the two of us, and, God willing, we'll end up the two of us.

With all my love,
Sarah

Richard thought to himself, *Now wait a minute.* Her son died and her husband had an affair in the past few years, and she sounded as though everything was fine. What was wrong with this picture?

He knew denial and other psychological defenses could protect people from the most painful of human experiences. But Richard also knew that his mother hadn't been like that. She hadn't avoided anything. She had faced whatever was taking place in her life at the time and had dealt with it directly. There had to be some other explanation for why she hadn't even mentioned the death or the affair.

He could add something else to the ideas of commitment and hope he'd identified a few minutes ago: courage. That was it.

His mother somehow had found the strength inside herself to move on.

She hadn't been about to stop being the mother of the four children who needed her. She had seemed to find the strength inside herself not only to move beyond Claire but to have the compassion not to rub her husband's face in the affair. At least not in an anniversary letter.

A competing interpretation entered Richard's consciousness. One that was less philosophical and less appreciative of his mother's sophistication.

He wondered if his mother's tone in this letter had been superficial.

After all, weren't these letters supposed to be open in their expression? The letter sounded as though almost nothing of significance had taken place. Maybe she wasn't being honest with her husband or herself.

If she was sweeping it under the rug, chances were good that they would trip over it at some point. Hopefully his father's letter would shed some light on the matter.

Dear Sarah,

I debated whether to write you this anniversary letter for
quite some time. Part of me wanted to keep it light and
simply loving and let it go at that. The other part of me is
convinced that intimacy is about being open and honest, and
I've decided to follow that lead as it has worked well for
us so far.

I want to thank you for finally not mentioning Claire
anymore. I know how much I hurt you and that the wound
hasn't just disappeared. I believe that you have decided to
move on, and I appreciate that. I realize that bringing her up
at all is risky, but I want to tell you some things.

An affair can tell you many things about yourself and
your life. Viewed on the surface, it might look like fun and
games. But I want you to know, Sarah, that my affair
made me realize not so much what I was missing in our
marriage but what I have.

I look at you after twenty years of marriage and still see
the woman I fell in love with. I believe that our love for each
other has grown into a mature one. Life and the demands it's
placed on us have tested us many times, and I believe we are
stronger for it. I hope you agree.

I also need to be honest about something else.

I continue to be deeply hurt over the loss of Peter. I pray
every night that our other children will be safe and protected. I
feel as though I somehow failed my son. I was 1,000 miles away

on a business trip meeting with some customers while my son drowned in a river. Why wasn't I there to protect him?

I don't care how irrational that sounds. I have this guilt that somehow I should have been there to save him. I fear that you may hold me responsible in some strange way. Isn't it the father's responsibility to protect his family? What I am about to write you, Sarah, will perhaps only make sense to me.

I am so sorry for Peter's death.

I love you and the children with all my heart.

Christopher

"Jesus Christ, Dad!"

Those words came out of Richard's mouth loudly enough for a few passengers to turn their heads.

He needed a minute or two to digest this one.

Richard searched inside himself, discovering many feelings at once. First and foremost, he thought about how painful it must have been for his father to carry this guilt and burden. Was he still feeling this way after all these years? He wanted to know.

But being a father, Richard also understood.

If you lost a child, you couldn't help blaming yourself, even if only in a minute way. Though the accident had absolutely nothing to do with his father, it still stood in the face of a prime directive: the primitive instinct to protect one's young.

Richard felt sad knowing his father suffered this way. He'd always been a good man. Devoted to his family. He shouldn't have suffered like this. Richard also realized something else.

His father wasn't without courage. He revealed his inner-most feelings to his wife, including those of the affair. Most everyone else Richard knew would have just kept his mouth shut and been thankful that it seemed over. But here was his dad bringing up Claire again. The idea that it made him appreciate his wife more was noble, but risky.

This letter, more than any other so far, made Richard realize how hidden from view their marriage really had been. In many ways, his parents had lived in a world that no one else knew about. Privacy had hidden their relationship—that is, until now.

A Quick Note

As he turned to the next page, Richard wondered what the following set of letters would hold. Instead of the usual set of exchanges, he found a plain white envelope paperclipped to the next few pages. The outside of the envelope contained some words in his father's handwriting.

In case of emotional overload, open envelope and read contents!

His dad always had a good sense of humor and it was good to see it especially at a time like this.

Richard took out the piece of plain white paper that had been carefully folded in half. The piece of gum wrapped inside it fell into his lap. He wasn't paying much attention to it, as the words in front of him were more important right now.

Hello, Richard,

Just a quick note. I trust you've found your reading both interesting and enlightening so far. It must be somewhat strange to see your parents as people, and I imagine that already you view us in a very different light. I hope that the letters are helpful to read.

But it's important you understand that these letters only capture the major themes of your mother's and my marriage. They cannot possibly express the thousands of moments that reflect the range of a life chosen together.

I want you to know that many hard moments came during even the best of our years together. The hard times also had moments of happiness.

You probably hardly remember us fighting at all. That's only because we believed that you children should be kept away from our problems. We vowed to show love in front of you but keep the conflicts between ourselves. Maybe that gave you the false impression that our marriage was perfect. I'm sorry if we did that.

By now you know how I felt about the loss of your brother

and how I dealt with it. I'm not proud of my actions, but have forgiven myself for them long ago. One of the advantages of aging, I think, is that we can forgive ourselves more, even if others cannot.

Richard, if after reading these letters you have further questions, you can call me anytime; just call soon, as I am getting older.

Also, if you want to share these letters with Laura, the answer is no.

I don't mind if you tell her that I gave them to you, but I want the contents kept between you and me. The only exception would be your sisters, as I've explained earlier.

You have turned out to be a wonderful son and I am very proud of you, as I am of your sisters.

So much for a quick note. If I know my son, then you're reading through all of these on the plane. Enjoy the rest of the flight.

Love,
Dad

PS: Though I haven't seen you do so in many years, as a child you almost always had a stick of gum in your mouth. It seemed to relax you. Just remember, there's more where that came from!

Richard thought to himself, *Dad's full of surprises, isn't he?* The offer to be able to talk about it was welcome, and he would definitely call his father later.

As far as Laura was concerned, he wasn't even thinking about sharing these letters with her. Dad was a great guy, but perhaps a bit too optimistic that these letters were going to turn anything around. They had made him reflect more, but that was about it.

Richard began unwrapping the gum and smiled to himself. It was a piece of Bazooka gum with the mini-comic story inside. He had lived on them when he was a kid. Long after the sweet taste of the sugar had gone, he'd chew on a single chunk for hours at a time.

As soon as Richard put the gum in his mouth, he experienced a strange link to his distant childhood. It was so long ago, but the taste of the gum was instantly familiar.

Reading the comic about Bazooka Joe, Richard felt a sense of comfort in knowing that some things don't seem to change. He was glad that his father had remembered after all these years.

Silver Anniversary

During the next few minutes, Richard found himself thinking about the last pair of anniversary letters. He saw in his practice how devastating grief could be.

He knew that grief was more than an emotion. It was a *force* that could overtake every fiber of your being. It seemed to penetrate every cell of your body and soul and could stay there forever.

Time was surely a powerful healer.

The pain would often subside, but under just the right circumstances the grief could come to the surface in a moment's time to remind you that the love was still there.

After all, at its deepest level, grief was love.

He hoped that year twenty-five would reveal a turn of life for the better.

Dear Sarah,

Our twenty-fifth anniversary is laced with silver and a big surprise, isn't it? Can you believe our baby girls are engaged? Twenty-two years old and they're both planning to be married. Didn't you and I just get married yesterday?

I'll never forget how they told us.

Sitting down for dinner on Wednesday evening, November 14. Routine conversation is about all I expected. I felt a little tense when Marcia announced, "I have something important to tell you all!" She was so serious.

A few thoughts quickly passed through my mind. She wasn't joining a commune or anything, was she? No. Not Marcia. She was too conservative for that.

Marie perhaps, but not Marcia.

God. Maybe she was pregnant. I dismissed that thought as being ridiculous considering she was a virgin. It's one of the illusions a father likes to hold onto about his daughters. Besides, if she was pregnant, she wouldn't be announcing that in front of the family.

The whole table became quiet as we fixed our eyes on her. "I'm getting married!" I didn't have a moment to process that when Marie chimed in, "Me too—next July!"

At that second I don't know who was more surprised— us or the twins. I wish I had a picture of the look on their faces as they looked at each other and began to laugh. It was news to them as well. Probably the only secret they'd kept to themselves.

I know I had a sinking feeling in my stomach: <u>Our babies weren't babies anymore.</u>

Announcing their engagements challenged my desire to hold onto the belief that they were my little girls, even at age twenty-two.

My own feelings quickly gave way to joy for them as we hugged. I was also thankful that Kenny and Robby are going to be our future sons-in-law. They're both good young men, and as parents, we can be so thankful for that.

I didn't know what else to say for the moment. I just sat back, slowly finishing my dinner and looking over at you. By now all the kids were jumping up and down in a frenzy of excitement.

Sarah, I saw the gleam in your eye. The tear that seemed to reveal your happiness and sadness all at once. We both knew without saying the words that another rite of passage was taking place, a marker in our lives together. It was a beginning and an end all at once.

It's ironic, isn't it? When they're young, you often wish they'd grow up so you could reclaim more of your own life. When it finally happens, part of you wants to go back in time.

You know, Sarah, in some ways it really doesn't matter what my views are on the twins getting engaged. The fact is life is moving on and we're getting older. Being forty-six years old didn't seem so bad until I realized I'd probably be a grandfather before too long. Time is moving forward too quickly, and it's a little scary.

I look upon all the children this year and want to praise you. I can appreciate more and more what a wonderful mother you've been. Raising four children hasn't been easy.

I know from our talks together how excited you are for the girls. I think you're being wise to keep some of your doubts about Robby to yourself. I agree that he's a bit immature, but I think he'll find his way in short order. Marcia will help him along with that, don't you think?

Well, I've rambled on a bit.

Before I finish, I want you to know that I've noticed you've made more of an effort to be affectionate this past year, and I appreciate it. I suppose it's like you said all along: As the children get older, you'll have more energy for us.

Happy anniversary (soon it will be happy anniversary, Grandma!).

Love,
Christopher

Richard felt some relief reading the positive tone of his father's letter. Five more years had gone by since the last entry and once again he wondered what had transpired during that time.

Richard was curious about why his father selected these years in particular for him to read. His father was a thoughtful man and he had carefully chosen which letters to reveal. Why hadn't he included year twenty-three or twenty-four? Or any of the other missing ones for that matter?

Richard doubted that the others were of lesser substance. If he had drawn one conclusion by this time, it was that his parents' marriage had been eventful. No year had been routine. Theirs had been a fluid relationship, not static like so many others.

Alive would be a good word to describe it.

Richard thought back to his father's introductory letter. In it, he had mentioned that earlier generations didn't talk openly about their problems. Reading these letters was triggering a great deal of curiosity about more than just his parents' marriage. He began to wonder about his grandparents' relationships and their parents'.

He had observed that so much history was lost forever over the generations these days. If you asked most people about their great-grandparents, they were unlikely to know anything at all—except, perhaps, where they had been born.

Then it occurred to him. He and Laura were potential great-grandparents at this very moment. A hundred years from now, would anyone know anything about him and Laura? Would anyone care?

It was important to have a familiar history. Yet Richard thought about how difficult it had become nowadays to find one's roots.

Different cultures. Different races. Different religions. Different sets of parents. Stepparents. Blended families. Single parents. One's history could easily become lost in the vortex of human relationships that was so different from the linear path previous generations had followed.

Richard was sure that these anniversary letters weren't intended to be historical documents. But in a sense, that's exactly what they were. The documentation of their marriage not only helped him understand his parents more intimately, but also showed him that their history was really a part of him.

He could now see for himself what they had experienced— their trials and tribulations; hopes and dreams; aspirations, expectations and disappointments. They all had to filter down through the children in some fashion.

Richard knew that in many ways we mirror our parents. It is a fact of life. *So, Mom, what do you have to say about the twins' engagements?* Richard surmised that it would probably dominate the theme of her letter as well.

Dear Christopher,

To say that this has been an eventful year in my life would be an extreme understatement. I had an affair this past year.

Richard put the letter down and shook his head from side to side in disbelief. He read the line again.

I had an affair this past year.

He placed his glasses carefully in his lap and looked out the window. He was expecting some nice sentimental entry that would essentially mirror many of his father's feelings. Now he was finding out that years ago his mother had an affair as well as his father. *Why now? With whom? Weren't they getting along better?*

His shock, Richard knew, was not because he felt judgmental. It was nothing like that. He knew that people have affairs—both men and women—for reasons that were human. Both his parents were very real, very human.

The surprise was more of the kind that takes place when you expect to open a box of chocolates and out pops a rabbit. Rabbits are fine, but you were expecting chocolates because that's what the box said all over it.

It was with a man you don't know and it lasted for about six months. Most of it took place while you were away on business.

It would shock you all the more, I think, because we seem to have done so well this past year. Well, Christopher, we did do better at times, but I tried to let you know I needed more of your attention. To feel like a woman again. And I needed something more.

I needed a friend. A confidant. I wasn't looking for it to happen, but it did. I was vulnerable.

You were increasingly preoccupied with your work.

I felt more and more caught in a rut that I suppose
finally caught up with me. I truly thought that I had
fully accepted the endless responsibilities of motherhood.
My needs for intimacy caught up with me.

Did I love him? No, Christopher. I've always loved
you and the affair helped me appreciate that even more.
In that way, my experience was not unlike yours with
Claire.

I am reluctant to tell you about the affair. I suspect I
am being a coward by hiding behind the notion that telling
you will cause unnecessary pain. I do feel guilty about what
I've done, but I know why I did it. I don't know if I'll
ever tell you.

It seems strange. You probably wouldn't have imagined
in a thousand years that I would have had an affair.
Well, up until it actually happened neither would I.

I think you stopped your affair with Claire because you
were caught. It took me some time, but I came to realize
that you loved me very deeply. I couldn't see it at the time,
but now it's clearer to me. I needed my relationship and
I also knew I would never leave you. It served its purpose
and I broke it off.

After twenty-five years of marriage, you're the man
I want to be with, Christopher. No fleeting fantasy will
separate us. No one from the outside can truly threaten

our bond. Only we have the power to do that. To blame another man or woman would be to look in the wrong place.

And affairs are fantasies, aren't they? Phantasms of an idea that fails to take into account real life.

The engagement of our twins is no postscript. I am so happy and proud. I look forward to seeing you walk them down the aisle, with some sadness, I admit.

I am proud of you as a husband and as a father.

All my love,
Sarah

Now what? Richard thought. Weren't his mother's reasons for having an affair the same as those Laura had claimed when she had hers? Laura had also said that she was lonely and looking for friendship. He felt that his mother's words were striking a little too close to home.

And what did these affairs mean? Did everyone have one at some point?

He understood, of course, that moral values notwithstanding, human needs were human needs. Richard saw it every day in his practice. One hundred percent of the time, people went outside the marriage because some need or needs weren't being met inside it. The desires for affection, understanding, intimacy and sex were basic.

He also saw that affairs could cause a great deal of hurt and damage to a relationship. Some couples could work through them, understand why they happened and move on. Others could not.

Still, he knew that imagining your mother and father with a respective boyfriend or girlfriend was hard to integrate as a child, no matter how old you were. These were *his* parents.

And who was this man with whom his mother had been involved? He would never know the answer to that question. At least his father's liaison could be attached to a name. He wondered how much it all bothered his father.

More questions surfaced in Richard's mind. Did his father let him see this letter so he would know his mother had cheated also? That she had evened the score, so that Richard would not judge his father too harshly for what happened with Claire?

No, he concluded, that wasn't it.

Richard realized instantly that his father trusted he would not judge them. It was a great deal of welcome confidence, considering Richard's mother had died just a little over a week ago.

Richard's father knew that his son could be trusted to honor his mother's memory. The letter was included to help him understand just how complicated things could get. But he also knew that it was more than that. His father wanted Richard to see that no person could break up his parents' marriage.

Richard had come to learn that their commitment was more powerful than anything or anyone else. If it could survive the death of a child, it could survive an affair.

Twenty-Sixth Year

The last letter would take some serious processing before he fully understood it, but now wasn't the time. Richard continued. The anniversary letters had a hold on him that pushed his reading forward.

The twins had married in the twenty-sixth year. They had decided to have a double wedding, and Richard had held the honor of being one of the ushers. He was eighteen years old then.

It was the first time he'd worn a tuxedo and he would always remember how tight the collar was. It was one of those details forever embedded in his memory.

He couldn't wait to loosen it at the reception. After the formalities of the pictures, first dances and cake, that's exactly what he did. That, and sneaking a few glasses of champagne while no one was watching.

His Uncle Steven had given the toast and he could still remember the gist of it now. It wasn't that his memory at eighteen was so accurate, it was the fact that his sister Marie liked the toast so much she had it embroidered and hung over her piano. She'd also given a calligraphic copy to each of her sisters and to Richard for Christmas presents a few years back. Marie had painstakingly lettered each copy herself.

It had come off Richard and Laura's bedroom wall one evening after a particularly bad fight. Not a mysterious disappearance but a deliberate act of anger by Richard himself. He later had regretted doing it, but Laura had not let him hang it up again. He remembered her exact words even now. "Let's not be hypocrites, Richard. We don't live that way, so why advertise to each other what we don't deliver?" Richard had been angry at the time but knew she was right.

Remember these words: Your marriages will offer you the opportunity of many happy times together. And there will also be times of private doubt. During the difficulties that will touch you along the way, remember this day and that your hearts brought you here for a sacred reason. There is no force on earth that can sever that bond if you both trust in each other's love.

Richard had always thought of it as a tasteful and realistic toast. Given the fact that Uncle Steven had been married thirty-four years at the time and was the father of six children himself, he spoke with some authority.

His twin sisters were both still happily married to Robby and Kenny. Suzanne was doing well also. Her husband Frank had been a friend of Richard's in college. In fact, Richard had introduced them to each other.

Their marriages weren't perfect, but they were working. He knew that because his sisters always confided in him. He told himself that was one of the advantages of being an only brother with three sisters: *they* confided all, and *he* saw all.

Sometimes he found it a little embarrassing to be such a trusted confidant. Richard never quite got over being seen by his high school buddies at the supermarket checkout line, holding a box of feminine napkins. His friends hadn't let him get over it too quickly either.

Suzanne had pleaded with him to go pick some up for her.

"Look, Richard, it will just take a minute. You'll be out in a flash. No one's going to see you or even care if they did."

"Okay, Sue, let's see if I've got this right. You'd go in and buy me a jockstrap in a pinch?"

"Of course, Richard. You're my brother. What size do you need?"

Richard always believed that growing up with his sisters gave him a distinct advantage over other men in terms of understanding women. On the other hand, he couldn't understand why, if he was such an expert on women, he was getting his second divorce.

Maybe he was a screw-up, but his sisters were obviously doing something right. Richard took some comfort in knowing that at least his siblings were successful in their relationships.

Dear Sarah,

Happy anniversary! Now that the twins are married, we'll have two more anniversaries to celebrate every year. Can you believe that we've been married twenty-six years? The time has gone by so quickly.

They both looked so beautiful. I have never felt so proud in my entire life. It was magical, mysterious and spiritual all at once for me. Our little girls are women, Sarah. But I know you've been aware of that for some time now. It's all part of a father's wish to preserve the myth that his little girls will always remain little girls.

Walking them both down the aisle was so special for me. It was a struggle to hold back the tears. I remember feeling the same way when the children were born. It's such a powerful moment.

This anniversary, I'm drawn to the remembrance of our own wedding.

I recall all the details as if it were yesterday. You looked so beautiful with your hair pulled back, eyes sparkling. Your dress was stunning but I mostly remember your eyes. They held such hope, such love and such expectations—as did mine. I saw those same eyes when I looked over at Marcia and Marie, as each exchanged vows with her husband-to-be.

Richard stopped reading for a moment. Recalling and reading about his sisters' wedding and his parents' inevitably led to Richard reflecting on his own.

Laura had looked beautiful that day. They had decided to get married in the evening. A friend had offered the balcony of his condominium on the twenty-eighth floor, overlooking Miami and the Atlantic Ocean. It was a warm, balmy evening in April.

Laura's blond hair had shone under the full moon above the Miami skyline. She had worn an off-white, ankle-length dress with a garland of flowers in her hair. No matter what had happened in their life together, Richard would never forget how beautiful she looked that evening.

He had been totally in love with her, completely swept away by the power and chemistry of their attraction to each other. It was one of those moments in time you wished could be frozen forever.

With all his complaining about Laura, he knew she had a certain softness to her, a sweet side that had been in full view on her wedding day. She had been happy then, too, and full of hope and expectation of a life together. Neither of them would have thought that they'd ever get a divorce. They'd both been married before; they were realistic and not naive. Or so they had thought.

Richard continued reading.

The reception was so much fun. But I do have to say that it was a strange experience to watch our girls dancing with their husbands. It was as though I were watching us in another time and place. Sarah, if Marie and Marcia find it in themselves to be anything like you as a wife and mother, they will be fortunate, as will their families. You can be proud.

We both know that they have many challenges ahead. Some they will be prepared to meet while others will catch them by surprise. Nothing can completely prepare one for marriage, can it? Each couple is unique, and at its deepest level, each marriage is a mystery unto itself.

We only see the tip of the iceberg, don't we? What we and others choose to show the outside world. The relationship, as it really is, mostly remains hidden from view.

I do worry about the world in which our children will be raising their own. There's just so much unnecessary conflict and we live in confusing times. This war in Vietnam— I hope it ends before Richard gets drafted. I pray for that. Kennedy's assassination over a decade ago. Racial tension. Changing roles for men and women. It all seems so overwhelming at times.

I don't know what is happening to our traditional values and morals. Change is inevitable, but it usually doesn't sweep through society this quickly. I suppose their generation will find its way.

In this, our twenty-sixth year of marriage, I find we have achieved a level of peace and understanding that we never had before. I think we are more accepting and less critical as time goes on.

We know each other very well at this point, Sarah. And yet there are still surprises at times. That's what keeps it interesting.

And we still do have our moments, don't we? Times of aggravation and frustration. We always will. In some ways, I think human beings are the slowest learners of all. We keep expecting things to change while applying the same strategy *each time—like trying to open a door using the wrong key again and again.*

Getting philosophical in my old age, aren't I? Well, my dear, have a wonderful anniversary.

Yours always,
Christopher

His father's words echoed the wishes of all loving parents, that their children have happy lives. But a deeper secret revealed itself between the words Richard had just read. It was a secret often unspoken, yet implicitly understood. *Parents want their children to have better lives than they had.*

Richard and Laura weren't an exception to that rule. They, too, were trying to improve on what they had grown up with as children. It was inevitable and it wasn't necessarily a criticism of their own upbringing. It was more like fulfilling a universal wish that as life went on the next generation would have it better than the one before.

Richard thought about what it would be like to see his own daughters married. In certain ways, his experience would be far different from his father's. By the time Christa and Sandi were married, Richard might be accompanied by another wife and Laura by a different husband. That would be strange enough.

The lifelong bond of having children together would in some ways be compromised by the presence of new spouses. If for no other reason than the welfare of the children, Richard surmised that he and Laura would likely be cordial.

Questions arose quickly in Richard's mind. They were the kind of questions that could play with your head if you let them.

How would the new spouses feel? How would the girls feel having their divorced parents there with new spouses? Would they harbor a secret wish that their parents were still together? What if one was remarried and the other wasn't? Would they all be seated together?

Richard concluded that there was no point in worrying about all that now. Many things could happen in the future.

It was just a shame that he and Laura wouldn't share such an important time in their children's lives.

There was something else Richard noticed.

In the earlier years, his mother seemed to be making a case for the "bigger picture." She emphasized the need to stay focused on the overall marriage. The hard times were part of the territory. Her letters, though kept to herself, helped give her comfort and strength.

His father's earlier letters were shorter and more to the point because he was reacting to life at the moment. When Richard thought about it, he realized it was one of the differences between his parents. His dad had more of a tendency to be impatient, while his mother took the longer view. Often, his impatience helped her to be more spontaneous, while she helped to settle him down. They balanced each other well.

In these later letters as his parents grew older, it seemed that his father came to see the bigger picture more clearly, while his mother no longer felt a need to explain her feelings quite as much.

Richard could also see that things were getting easier for

them. The house was thinning out, which reduced some of the responsibilities and chores of parenting. He could appreciate that raising four children took a lot of energy.

Now that's the understatement of the century, Richard thought. He couldn't for the life of him understand how his mother's parents had taken care of eight children.

Children were a responsibility unlike any other. That was a matter of fact, not opinion. They required a level of care that forced you to put your own needs as an individual or as a couple on the proverbial back burner. The problem was that the back burner could die out if no one watched it.

He'd seen many couples split up after the children were grown. This usually happened because the parents felt an obligation to stay together because of the children. In very dysfunctional marriages, they weren't doing anyone a favor.

Richard saw that other marriages ended when children left because the presence of the children served as a buffer, an insulation that protected the couple from confronting their unhappiness. Of course, the vast majority of individuals in previous generations simply didn't view divorce as an option.

The successful couples were either better matched from day one, or they had mastered the basic principles of mutual respect and understanding.

Richard turned the page to reveal a card from his mother. A small yellow Post-it was attached to the front and contained a short line in his father's handwriting.

Richard,

This is a card I received from your mother on our twenty-sixth anniversary.

"Happy Anniversary" was written in fancy script on the cover.

There was a picture of a couple, taken from behind, walking along a beach hand in hand. The man had on a pair of khaki pants that were rolled up and the bottoms were wet from the surf. His red shirt provided a nice contrast to the deep blue of the ocean beyond.

The woman in the picture wore a simple, knee-length white skirt and a loose-fitting white sweater. In the background, the sun was setting and it seemed to push them to the foreground of the photograph.

It was an idyllic scene. The perfect couple walking along the perfect beach at the perfect time of day with, no doubt, the perfect relationship.

These cards are so damn unrealistic, Richard thought. *Don't tell me Mom bought a card with a corny inscription inside every year.*

He opened the card. Taped to the left side was a small, dried flower. The petals had deteriorated completely and he couldn't tell what kind of flower it was. A freshly applied strip of cellophane covered both the tape and what was left of the flower.

On the right, he recognized his mother's handwriting. The corny commercial inscription he'd predicted would be there was missing. It was a blank card with a nice picture on the front.

Dear Christopher,

I need to tell you something. It is so important, so vital that you know. Take these words into your heart and soul. Read them carefully.

This flower was picked by me in a field next to the beach in Carmel this past weekend. Look carefully at the petals. As beautiful as they are, they will fall away. But now look at the stem. Its strength will remain as it supports the beauty of the petals.

Our time on this earth will come and go as it does for all living things.

You have been my core, Christopher, and hopefully I've been yours. Your love for me has seen me through many hard times and has not gone unnoticed.

Thank you for coming into my life.

Love,
Sarah

Simple, kind words of love and appreciation. Richard knew they came from her heart.

He and Laura used to write this kind of card to each other early in their relationship. They wrote about love also. After a few years, the writing became less expressive and, upon reflection, more dishonest.

Signing a card "all my love" didn't mean anything if your actions didn't reflect it. The cards Richard and Laura had exchanged in the past few years were perfunctory more than anything else, an obligation rather than an affirmation.

It seemed sad to Richard that he and Laura hadn't taken the time to write each other a few lines every year about their marriage. Even if it was as simple as expressing compassion to each other about their having a hard time. Empathy doesn't have to mean unconditional alliance. If each of them had acknowledged the other was hurting, it might have helped things. It certainly couldn't have done any harm.

What was our excuse anyway? Richard wondered. His parents had found the time and energy. They must have felt adversarial on at least a few occasions when they wrote to each other.

In reading this card, though, Richard could see that in some ways Laura was much like his mother. She had a romantic side. Wasn't Laura the one who had referred to their marriage as a union of soul mates? Laura also had a core of faith in the marriage, especially during the early years.

But ultimately, the fundamental differences in the way they viewed their marital problems helped bring their relationship to an end.

Richard saw the marriage as one that had turned into an unhappy, mutually unfulfilling relationship. Laura believed the problems were serious but part of a phase that they would get through in years to come. It was a fundamental difference in perspective, but in a sense they were both right.

There was still more to read from the twenty-sixth year.

Dear Christopher,

What a milestone year this has been in our lives. Before I reflect on the children, there is something else that needs to be said.

Before reading the next line, Richard felt a bit anxious. For a split second, he was afraid some secret was about to reveal itself, one that would complicate this special time in his parents' lives. He hoped that wouldn't be the case. They'd been through so much already.

I believe that we are entering a new phase in our marriage. One that will give us more of an opportunity to regain our friendship. We have expended so much time and energy over the years and, as you know from many of our talks, I've always viewed it as a huge responsibility and a privilege.

There is certainly a lot of work ahead, but it is already so much easier. We have time to ourselves and that is a luxury. We can actually make love in the afternoon on a Saturday without the children pounding on the door. How's that for a treat?

I want us to get to know each other better. There are so many things one takes for granted in a marriage. I want us to take the time to learn about us again, the way we did when we were dating and were first married.

In many ways, I've missed you over the years, Christopher. I look back and see that our conflicts have always arisen because our needs weren't being met.

When I was younger, I used to see conflict as a negative thing. Something to be avoided. In my own naive way, I thought that the perfect marriage was one in which no conflict took place. Experience has taught me something else.

Conflict is natural in a relationship. It seems to come mostly from needs that go unfulfilled. My grandfather used to say he was suspicious of a relationship in which no fighting ever took place. Now I know what he meant.

I am glad we found the strength inside ourselves to make it through these past few years together. Some of them were especially difficult, and at the time I'm sure we both felt things wouldn't get any better. But they did.

I want you to know how much I appreciate you, Christopher. You continue to be a wonderful father and husband.

As for the wedding, I couldn't help but think about how strange it was that it seemed to me just the other day I was walking the twins through the park, showing them off to whomever showed interest. They were babies then. Now,

they're grown women starting lives on their own. Soon
they will be proudly showing off their own children.

There are so many memories a mother and daughter
share. I worked hard to have a special relationship with all
the children, though it was especially challenging to do so
with the twins. It was sometimes hard to separate them into
individuals, but the uniqueness of their personalities helped.

We had some trying times during their adolescent years.
They struggled with their young adulthood and asserted
their independence. It was a special kind of defiance that
mothers and daughters experience. We seem to have come
through it with minimal bruises, I think.

Suzanne and I are going through some of the same
trials right now, but that's all right. Richard and I get
along fine, but I see the two of you struggling for
dominance sometimes. He has your spirit, Christopher,
and he respects you and loves you very much.

Our nest is beginning to empty. I confess that I feel
some sadness as our children grow into adults. It's a
natural emotion, one that I'm sure all parents feel.

All in all, our purpose is changing and I am optimistic
about the future.

All my love,
Sarah

No surprises this year, Richard thought. *Thank God for that.*

It was good to see that both his parents had arrived at a place that offered them a measure of peace. That was true for them as individuals and as a married couple.

Reflections

ichard put the letters down. He had
been reading for two straight hours,
and it was a lot for his mind to
absorb.

He was trying to understand the meaning of it
all. The letters had transcended time and space
and it seemed as though all the events compressed
and were happening right now.

In a strange way, he felt as though the letters demanded some kind of a response; some reaction.
They were too powerful to simply ignore and pass
off as a nice remembrance of his father and mother.

Richard glanced around the cabin in front of
him. The plane was nearly full and there was
the usual cross-section of passengers on board, a
collection of strangers who all had stories to
tell. He thought about how each one had his or
her own history, joys, disappointments and

sorrows. He wondered how many were single, married, widowed, or remarried.

An older couple from his parents' generation was sitting directly across the aisle from him. How long had they been married? Did they have children? Grandchildren? And the million-dollar question: Were they happy? Farther up the aisle, he saw a young couple in what appeared to be their early twenties holding hands and laughing. *Probably married a short time*, he thought. Maybe they were even returning from their honeymoon; the flight had originated in Hawaii.

Richard imagined that these two couples were on opposite ends of the marriage continuum. One couple just starting out and the other nearing the end. He knew that statistics would argue against the younger couple making it all the way. It seemed so strange to him that two people could be so convinced of a lifetime commitment to each other, only to have it unravel somewhere down the line.

The other couples on the plane who were neither newlyweds nor older appeared to be the most distant. He could observe little conversation and no affection. Richard thought that perhaps married couples universally experienced the early and later years of marriage as the happiest and the middle years as the most difficult.

It would stand to reason. Personally and professionally, he'd seen over and over again that the middle years were the ones where children, work and the demands of life most severely challenge the marriage. It was a time when couples became lost in their routine and felt neglected.

Hadn't his own parents' letters illustrated just that fact? The early years were fun, full of hopes and dreams. As time went on, it became more difficult to feel the magic that had brought them together.

Upon closer inspection, he was coming to some deeper insights based on these observations. He realized that the anniversary letters were really about how a loving relationship matures over time. Life and its demands simply wouldn't permit his parents' love for each other to remain naive and immature. If their relationship was to survive, they had to make room for the changes that invariably accompany a long-term relationship.

Richard realized that only a wise couple will be insightful enough to see these demands as the price that necessarily accompanies commitment. A strong marriage would get through it and by now it was clear that his father and mother had a strong marriage.

Questions arose that only Richard himself could answer: *What did I expect when I married Laura, anyway? Did I really think we would always continue to make love on the kitchen counter or living room floor without interruption? Why didn't anyone clue me into the fact that children have a way of knowing just when to bang on a bedroom door when Mom and Dad are having sex? What made me think that Laura and I would always look into each other's eyes over a glass of wine, share our philosophy of life and see the reflections of each other's souls?*

"For better or worse," Richard thought, *we had actually said those words. Perhaps the phrase should be changed to "for better and for worse." It's more realistic.*

Richard was well aware that their marriage had become a love-hate relationship. The disagreements they had became heated arguments and understanding had given way to resentment. The roller-coaster relationship they both found themselves in had become impossible to handle. They were both exhausted and wanted it to end.

Richard had concluded that they were just a bad match— not completely, just in certain critical areas that made it impossible for them to stay together.

He remembered describing their differences to a colleague one evening over dinner. "It's like I see our marriage as a Mercedes-Benz and she sees it as a Toyota. Laura thinks you tighten up a relationship bolt here and there every ten thousand miles or so and it should run forever. I think it's got to be kept finely tuned at all times.

"For the life of me, I can never figure her out. She just doesn't think like anyone else I know. It's a never-ending challenge and frustration."

His friend had offered an insight: "Perhaps that's part of what attracted you to Laura, Richard. The challenge of being with someone who is anything but boring."

Richard responded, "I used to believe that, but the challenge became less and less interesting over time, while the frustration became more and more unbearable."

Richard's thoughts turned to a consideration of what reading these letters was doing to him. He was seeing his parents' marriage in a different light. It was a view from the inside that his father so generously offered him. It was a picture that, as a child, he could never have seen.

With each anniversary year, he could feel the complexity of their relationship further develop. His parents' relationship was much more involved than he ever gave it credit for being. He knew that it could never again be dismissed as a simple marriage.

Their superficial expectations had given way to the deeper value of commitment—a commitment that life had tested.

Richard also saw more clearly that it was not only Laura's expectations, but also his own that were getting in their way. Laura wasn't the problem; they *both* were. This wasn't a new revelation; the anniversary letters were just making the point clearer. He could see much of himself in his father's words and much of Laura in his mother's.

"Excuse me, would you like some chicken?" Richard looked up. The older man seated directly across the aisle turned toward him. "My wife and I are vegetarians. Would you like my entree?"

Richard saw an opportunity and quickly seized it. He wasn't interested in the chicken but was curious about their marriage. He was searching for answers to questions he had considered settled two hours ago. Perhaps he could gain some insight from these complete strangers who happened to be sitting near him. It was easy for Richard to draw people out—that is, everyone but Laura.

"Newlyweds?" Richard smiled.

"Not quite!" the woman answered. "We'll be married fifty-three years in May." Richard guessed that she was around his own mother's age.

Her gray hair was cut short, giving her an energetic and youthful appearance. Her face was weathered with age but her blue eyes still sparkled. He knew in an instant, by studying her face, tone of voice and smile, that this woman was still very full of life.

"What's the secret?" he asked. The couple exchanged a glance. The man answered first. "Tolerance. Don't let the differences bother you so much."

"Simple enough," Richard responded. *Perhaps too simple*, he thought. Richard hoped for a more detailed answer from the man's wife, but she followed her husband's lead. "Love is the most important thing. When you realize that you love someone to the depths of your heart, everything else is unimportant."

Richard's mental reaction was immediate. *Sounds too much like a Hallmark card*. Going through a divorce made him skeptical; still, they sounded so sincere. After fifty-three years together, they were no doubt doing something right.

"And you? Is Miami home?" Her tone of voice carried with it a sense of genuine interest.

"Yes." Anticipating the next question, Richard volunteered, "Just out in California for a business meeting." He saw no need to tell them the real reason for the trip. He wasn't in the mood to trigger any more grief.

"And how about you?" the man asked. "You married?" Richard paused for a moment. "Yes, fifteen years."

"Any children?" the woman was quick to add.

"Two girls, eleven and nine."

"That's wonderful. Do you have a picture?" the woman asked.

Richard automatically reached for his wallet. In the time it took him to pull out the picture, he found himself wishing he'd just said he didn't have any pictures with him. But it was too late for that.

The older couple studied the photograph carefully. It was a wallet-size copy of a family portrait taken a year and a half ago. Richard and Laura were standing on either side of Christa and Sandi. Richard looked handsome in his dark blue suit and Laura was beautiful in her black dress.

Christa's blond hair was hanging down freely over her shoulders and she was wearing a soft pink dress that matched her sister's. Sandi's brown hair was pulled back into a bun and both girls were smiling broadly.

"You and your wife make a lovely couple," the woman said. "And your girls are absolutely adorable. I think the older one looks more like your wife, while the younger one looks more like you."

""What do you think, Jack?" she asked her husband.

"Absolutely, Betty," he answered, as he reached over the aisle to return the picture to Richard. "I'll bet you hear that all the time."

"On occasion," Richard replied with a smile.

Betty leaned over Jack and said to Richard, "Two of our granddaughters are around that age. It's hard to keep track, though. We've got—what? Sixteen grandchildren in all?" She looked to her husband for confirmation.

Before he had a chance to respond, Betty reached into her pocketbook to pull out a small photo album. She was obviously proud as she worked her way quickly through pages of family photos. She went at just the right speed so as to keep interest. Richard could tell that she had gone through these pictures many times before, and he felt a sense of privilege as she shared this piece of her personal life with a stranger.

"Sounds a little too simple, doesn't it? I mean, our view of marriage." The woman could somehow sense that he wasn't convinced; she seemed to know what was on his mind.

A bit surprised by her perceptiveness, Richard responded, "Yeah, I'm afraid it does. Life is much more complicated these days, with so many frustrations and pressures. People seem to do more and more and get less and less satisfaction from it all."

What did this couple know, anyway? Richard thought. *They were out of touch with the pressures of modern-day life.*

"You know what my father told me a long time ago when I first got married? 'Commitment will set you free and doubt will undermine the mission,'" Jack interjected.

"The mission?" Richard was a little confused. The man continued. "When my father told me that, I had no idea what he was talking about. But later in life, I figured it out. The mission is to raise happy, healthy children and to love and honor your mate. Be there for your friends and add something of value to the world. After that, there's nothing left in life that's important."

"I'll have to give that some more thought," Richard replied.

After a few more moments of small talk, the flight attendants picked up the trays and the in-flight movie began. The cabin became quiet as the flight continued its eastward journey.

Richard settled into that quiet time during a plane trip, when this most unnatural experience—flying 550 miles per hour at 35,000 feet, inside a hollow metal tube—created a peaceful feeling.

He couldn't explain it, but that brief exchange helped him feel more centered. This older couple had a gentle air of relaxation about them that radiated comfort. It was good to know some couples could be happy together after so many years.

Richard felt a sense of inner peace as he turned on the overhead light and picked up the letters to begin reading once again.

Year Thirty-One

A turn of the page and time jumped from year twenty-six to thirty-one. Five more years of marriage had passed, and Richard himself was now in his early adult years, a young man of twenty-three with a life ahead of him.

Richard had finished his undergraduate schooling two years before and had been accepted to medical school. He'd lived at home and commuted to the local university while working part-time to subsidize his education. He also had become engaged that December to his high school girlfriend. Later that year, they planned to get married.

Richard now thought about his first wife, Cindy. It was common terminology nowadays, wasn't it? First wife. Second husband. Third wife. Fourth husband. A sort of serial marital bond.

Cindy had been totally devoted to him. Though they both had been young and immature, she had tried to be the best wife she could be.

In truth, Richard had caused the demise of his first marriage. He just hadn't been ready. If he hadn't rebelled, they would still be married today. That much he knew for certain.

Richard had met Cindy at age seventeen. It was the only serious relationship he'd had with a girl. He didn't really count the brief summer tryst he'd had while away at camp two summers before. That hadn't been a relationship; it had been pure lust.

The pressures medical school brought to bear on their marriage had not helped. Fourteen-hour days of classes and studying had been routine. Weekends had meant merely more study time. Looking back, Richard realized that this was a recipe for failure in any marriage, unless both partners were truly committed to the long run.

Cindy and he had fought all the time, but he couldn't remember about what. It seemed so long ago now and their marriage lasted just under two years.

Richard still would have an occasional dream about her. The content of the dreams usually concerned some pleasant event during their dating years in high school. It was a nice regressive gift from his unconscious mind to remind him of a simpler and happier time in his life. On other occasions, he'd dream about something contemporary, as though he were still married to her.

At times, his remembrances of Cindy raised those "what if" questions. What if they'd stayed married, survived medical school together and had a few children? Would he have been ultimately better off than he had been with Laura?

He had realized many years ago that life was full of "what ifs."

Richard thought about some of the similarities that existed between Cindy and Laura. Both women had strong personalities. They both were bright and had career interests. But there the similarities ended. Cindy was traditional and Laura was anything but.

A lifetime with Cindy would have been ordered, predictable and honestly boring. Richard wasn't blaming her; it was them as a couple. They were perhaps too similar. He and Cindy both originally came from suburban Long Island, products of post-war Catholic families. They grew up in the same town and had many of the same friends. Their fathers both worked for Grumman Aircraft and had been transferred to San Francisco at the same time. They had similar interests and habits. And there was something else that characterized their relationship: no challenge.

Richard's marriage with Laura, on the other hand, may have been a lot of things, but it never had been boring. It had been more like a roller-coaster ride with few smooth turns, as he'd previously reflected. The ups were high while the downs were the pits.

Whenever Richard thought about the good times, he would think about how they had often stayed up into the early hours of the morning. They would drink some wine, make love, talk about anything and everything, and laugh a lot.

Richard remembered how Laura could make him laugh. She had a great sense of humor and a quick wit that had him rolling off the bed sometimes.

She also had an unpredictable side to her. He remembered her excusing herself once to go into the bathroom late one

evening when they had been lying in bed. After a few minutes, she had emerged wearing a jet-black wig, high heels and
a fringed black negligee. She looked more like a hooker than
a Harvard-educated attorney.

Richard remembered that the truly amazing part was how
she had acted as cool as a cucumber, as though nothing at all
was different about her. Ten minutes before she had been a
blond in an oversized T-shirt and then she had transformed
herself into a seductress who looked nothing at all like
"Laura." She had played out the fantasy to the hilt, ignoring
Richard's astonishment.

He truly missed those times. Of course they had their share
of down times too. Overall, the ride had been fun for a while,
but after some time he had wanted to trade the ride in for some
relationship *terra firma*. The smooth predictability of routine
was something Richard found himself longing for at times.

Richard had always known that his parents were traditional
in their values. The letters revealed that, in spite of that, they
certainly had an eventful marriage. They seemed to have kept
it interesting. Life kept it interesting—sometimes in very
unwelcome ways.

Richard thumbed through the now thinning stack of
papers in his lap. Ten or so pages remained. According to the
overhead announcement, they would be on the ground in
Miami in another ninety minutes. It was more than enough
time to complete his reading.

He knew that he could always finish them later, but he
wanted to finish them now. By the time he arrived in Miami,
Richard wanted to have gone through all of them once. After
that, there would be plenty of time to reread them.

Dear Sarah,

Well, I can honestly say that this year has been one of mixed feelings for me. Richard's leaving home last August caught me by surprise. I thought that the other children leaving one by one had given me enough experience at separation. I was caught off guard.

I am so happy for his engagement to Cindy. She is such a sweet girl and comes from a good family. I'm certain they'll be happy together. Richard could use the stability. He's so restless and reminds me of myself at his age.

Along with you, I miss the earlier years at times. Strange how when they're small and demand so much of your time and energy you wish they'd grow up and be less dependent. Then, one day they walk out the door and they're adults. A natural course of events that feels so unnatural to a parent.

I know I shouldn't be saying this, but Richard has a special place in my heart. I love all the children equally; you know that. It's just that we have that special father-son relationship that I always dreamed of having when I first thought about becoming a father. I know you understand this because of your special mother-daughter relationships.

Now, in this, our thirty-second year together, we're going to be on our own again. It's hard to believe that we've had twenty-eight years of continuously having children in our home.

Sarah, when I look back at all our years together, I think we should give each other credit for a job well done. I've always thought of raising children as one of the most challenging missions a man and woman can undertake in their lifetimes.

I now know that to be a fact rather than an opinion.

Is it crazy to believe that shaping a human being into someone who has the potential to touch the world in meaningful ways is a privilege? Of course not. I've also come to another conclusion.

As long as children know that they are loved, without conditions, it's hard to screw them up.

That doesn't mean that I wouldn't have done many things differently if I could go back in time. But that's true for all of us.

I would have found more time for them—time to enjoy the most commonplace moments more. I would have scolded less and listened more. But such is the nature of life; we would do many things differently if we had the opportunity.

My own father was very loving but found it difficult to say the words often enough. As a result, all his children knew how much he cared by his actions more than his words. Saying it just wasn't his way.

Still, nothing is so powerful as the spoken words "I love you." Words leave no doubt or question, as actions sometimes do. We both told the children openly that we loved them and these words flowed freely around our family.

I think the words have been absorbed into the walls of our home many thousands of times. All four children can express it freely. They have good, solid, moral beliefs concerning how to treat others, yet they know not to let anyone take advantage of them. I know that in many ways they are better equipped than you and I were when we started out.

As for you, young lady, you have always been and continue to be a wonderful mother—and grandmother, I might add. Our four grandchildren—David, Dawn, Tracy and Corrine—adore you. How many more can we predict to join the clan in the years to come?

Here comes the mushy part. I want you to read each word slowly, roll it around in your mind until you've carefully digested its meaning. Here it comes.

I love you more now than the day I married you. My happiness has grown under the influence of your gentle nurturing. My commitment is complete and can go no deeper. I admire your beauty, intelligence, wit and exemplary ability as a lover.

Yes, honey. I find you very sexy and, if you play your cards right, I might just let you take advantage of my body, which is always on call for your sensual delights.

I'm yours now and always.

Love,
Christopher

Richard smiled. His dad apparently had a healthy libido.

The earlier part of the letter evoked a sense of happiness as Richard learned of his father's deep feelings for him. He appreciated the sentiments his father shared as he knew many people would spend their lives never knowing how their parents felt about them.

That was one area in which Richard felt that he and Laura had done a good job. As parents, they were on the same page and never argued about how to raise the children. Most important, Richard knew, was the fact that Sandi and Christa felt loved by both of them.

Laura was an excellent mother. She was devoted to the girls and was raising them with good, solid values of respect for others and appreciation for what they had. Richard felt disappointed in himself at times because he didn't have as much patience or dedication as a parent as Laura had. He let the demands of his career get in the way sometimes.

Even so, Laura always acknowledged that he was a good father and Richard was grateful for that.

They both also had agreed that during and after the divorce they would try to get along as civilly as possible for the sake of the girls. Time would tell if they would achieve that goal.

Richard began reading his mother's letter.

Dear Christopher,

Happy anniversary. I can hardly believe it's really over. We've raised all our children and the last one has left the nest. Seeing Richard pull out of the driveway in his overloaded VW bug, I imagined myself a mother bird watching her offspring's first flight. I wanted to believe that it was just a test flight to see if he could fly alone. My fledgling would awkwardly try to achieve grace in the air, flop about a little but finally return to the safety of the nest.

But, of course, humans aren't like that. We will see Richard again on his occasional weekend at home. And probably even less so once he and Cindy are married.

How could anyone even hope to slow down nature? Wanting to is a natural parental reaction to a process over which we no longer have control. And so it goes.

As a mother it is hard to describe how I feel, but I'll try. I know that as a father you feel some sense of loss, but it's different for a mother. Each and every mother knows what I mean. We all experience it in our gut.

You see, Christopher, since I was a little girl I'd always dreamt of marrying and raising a family. I played with dolls that were characters in my new family. My friends and I fantasized for hours. My mother told me that she played the same way when she was a little girl, as her own mother did.

We girls grow into young ladies and embark on a path that leads us to become women. A one-way evolution pushes us forward in an effort to meet someone and mate.

And then, if you are fortunate enough, your marriage fulfills some of your expectations. Some, but not possibly all.

I married a wonderful man and had the honor and the privilege of raising four wonderful children.

The events in our life turned a painful course for the worse with Peter's death. Had he lived, I know in my heart how proud of him we would have been as well. Still, I don't know about you, Christopher, but Peter's death taught me about the fragility of life. Since that horrible day years ago, I have never taken any aspect of my life for granted. That is especially true when it comes to appreciating my children and my husband.

The loss of Peter will always be a tragedy, but his spirit lives on in the lives of those who were closest to him. Sometimes when I look closely, I see hints of his personality in all of us. I see much of him in Richard especially.

I look back at the last few lines I've put to pen and realize I must need to get some feelings out about Peter. Well, I'm glad I did and I know you feel much the same. Now for the rest of my thoughts.

Raising a family became the challenge of my lifetime.

There may not seem to be any glory in forever washing clothes by hand, mending tears, attending to bruises and cooking. But for me, I became an important thread in the fabric that held together our family life.

And it was far more than that.

It was about talking to the girls late at night and

drying their tears when their hearts were breaking over
their first loves. Of caring for them when they were sick.
Of helping Richard to understand you better. Of guiding
all of them through the early parts of their lives.

Traditional motherhood seems to be coming under attack
these days. Many women are pursuing careers that were
never open to them before.

I think all these developments for women are wonderful,
and I'm glad we pushed all our girls to receive formal
educations. But there's something else I know.

Suzanne loves her career, but she doesn't have a family
yet. I predict that she and millions of women who enter
the workforce will find themselves with two hectic full-time
jobs. I believe that women who choose the career path and
elect to have a child will experience even more stress than
I did. Even though the family size has dropped, the
responsibility for child care, school, meals, doctor appoint-
ments, family budgeting and many other responsibilities
will rest with the wife. I hope I'm wrong about this.
I just worry, that's all.

So many women are on their own today as single
parents, and it frightens me. No support whatsoever. An
unbalanced family that the mother tries desperately to
nurture while working two jobs.

And at least when I was raising our children, I had

help and advice from my family. My sister lived two doors down and she had three of her own. Besides, I could always count on Aunt Kim to watch the kids in a pinch. I honestly don't know how I could have made it through Peter's death without the support of my family and Mary.

We grew up in a neighborhood with identity and soul. I fear our children will be more isolated. We'll just have to support them as much as possible.

On the other hand, I do at times wish I had pursued a career of some kind. Now that Richard has moved out, I have even more time on my hands. My chores go by quickly and I sometimes find myself peering out the front window in anticipation of one of the children coming home. It's complicated.

I am happy to have such good friends in my life. I think that even beyond children the most important mark we can make in this lifetime is the way we touch and treat others. I plan to put more energy into my friendships, including ours.

I want you to know, Christopher, that I deeply appreciate all you have done for me and for the children over the years. The family was always well provided for and we never did without.

One of your qualities I admire most is your selfless devotion to our family.

Well, looking over what I've written this year, it's not a very romantic anniversary letter, I dare say. Perhaps this is my turn to get a little philosophical: the musings of a mother experiencing what Richard read in his psychology text as "the empty nest syndrome."

I love you, baby,
Sarah

Richard realized, even more so in reading this past letter, that he had never given his mother enough credit for how smart she had been. He had always viewed her as intelligent and having an abundance of common sense. But this was different.

She had been insightful and had a handle on what was important in life. In fact, both his parents wrote letters that tended to be philosophical. It was an essential ingredient that had helped them through some difficult times.

Richard himself strongly believed that all people needed a philosophy of life to support their actions. A sense of purpose was something that had pushed his parents out of bed each day to face another sixteen hours of often thankless work. Their own needs were lost in a sea of responsibilities as was their marriage at times. You needed something to sustain you.

Richard thought perhaps that was the problem with a lot of relationships today. They lacked clear direction and purpose. All around him he saw that when people didn't have a strong philosophy to help them understand life better, they'd find themselves quitting or leading a mediocre existence.

Richard could see that his parents' marriage had matured to the point of acceptance and increased patience with each other. There also had emerged a growing respect and appreciation for each other. It was clear that neither partner had been alone in experiencing disappointment or frustration. No competition about who was right and who was wrong existed any longer. The letters were now about understanding the bigger picture. Their love for each other had become truly selfless.

Richard also knew that divorcing Laura would eliminate the possibility of their ever being together again.

He knew that some couples remarried, but he and Laura never would. When they divorced, it would be over forever. It was in both of their personalities to grieve but then move on.

Year Forty

In the nine years that had passed since the last set of letters, a number of events had taken place. The birth of Suzanne's two sons and Marie's daughter brought three new grandchildren into the family.

Richard and Cindy had divorced, and he and Laura had married and become parents with the births of Sandi and Christa. He wondered if his father had carefully avoided any anniversary letters that made references to his and Cindy's divorce. Richard knew that his parents had felt hurt and disappointed, but they had kept it to themselves.

Now that Richard was a parent himself, he understood that it was easy enough to take the problems and failures of one's children to heart. It seemed as though you were deficient in some way as a parent.

He really hoped his parents hadn't felt that way. Over the years, he'd seen their tendency to take the accomplishments and disappointments of their children personally.

A short cover note preceded his father's next letter.

Dear Sarah,

Before you read this year's anniversary letter, there's something I'd like you to do. Please follow these instructions.

I want you to read this letter at around four in the afternoon. Make yourself a cup of tea and sit in your favorite chair on the back porch.

Ready?

Now take a deep breath and use your imagination. I want you to imagine it's forty-three years ago and you and I are on the front porch of your parents' house. I am eighteen and you are seventeen. It's late afternoon, the sky is bright blue and a soft, gentle breeze is flowing through the oak tree on the front lawn. The sun is reflecting off the leaves and for the moment all time stands still.

Now close your eyes and see in your mind's eye that time and place. Once you have a good picture in your mind, turn the page and read my letter to you.

Richard tried his best to imagine the scene himself. He wondered what his parents must have been like when they had been that young and full of life and expectation.

Without more details of the scene to rely on, he let his imagination fill in the gaps. At least he remembered what his grandparents' porch had looked like. He and Peter used to play outside all the time when they visited on weekends. The planks would creak under their shoes as they ran up the steps to go inside for a snack or to cool off.

The summers on Long Island were the hottest he'd ever experienced in his life. It was the summer heat that comes with a child's energy. Nothing, not even the heat of August in Miami, would ever come close to it.

He could imagine his mother following these instructions and wondering, as he was now, what his father's letter would reveal.

I remember one afternoon in the spring of 1945. I sat next to you on the porch while your parents were inside. We were kissing and holding hands and I hoped we wouldn't get caught.

I brushed your hair back over your shoulders. It was so long then. I pulled you nearer and whispered "I love you" in your ear. I'd been planning to tell you how special you'd become to me but I realized in that instant that it was more than that.

Later on that evening, I told my father, and I remember him telling me that a first love was always exciting. I told him you would be my only love. Time has proved me right. It usually doesn't happen this way, but it did for us.

It was a magical moment for me. Sometimes it seems to me that life comes down to your memories, especially when you get older. It was a moment that I have always cherished.

There have been times over the past forty years of marriage that I tried to find that magic and couldn't. In the darkest times of our relationship, my fear was that it was gone forever, that it was something young people in love have that later disappears. I wanted to go back to that simpler time and relive the excitement and the love I felt.

I want you to know something else, Sarah. The magic has always been there. At times it may have been buried deeper than I could dig for it, but it was always there. The magic matured with the reality that marriage and raising a family bring. Now that our lives have slowed down somewhat, I can finally take the time to enjoy you more. New experiences still await us. We finally have time to explore things we never could up until now.

I believe that in the past few years we have become closer than we had been for some time. I want you to know that I look at you when you don't know it. And I see the beauty and purity of that seventeen-year-old soul I fell in love with.

Sometimes forty-three years ago is just a moment away.

Love,
Christopher

Richard made a mental note to himself that he must tell his father what a good writer he was and how romantic his words were. His father had always had a tough and a soft side. Strict, but gentle when you needed him to be. The emotions didn't surprise him as much as his father's ability to articulate them.

He could easily identify with his father's sentiments about time. As Richard got older he also found himself thinking more and more about the past. That was especially true now that he and Laura were getting a divorce. Memories of her and the children seemed to preoccupy him at times. Under the circumstances he couldn't help it.

One of his fondest memories was of a weekend cruise they'd taken as a family from Miami to the Bahamas. Sandi and Christa must have climbed up and down the bunk beds above Richard and Laura's berths a hundred times.

They had all laughed so hard when, after the lifeboat drill, they kept bumping into each other in their oversized life jackets.

Laura had started it. They'd come back into the cabin after the drill. She'd given Richard a playful shove, and the challenge had begun. He had pushed back and the children had giggled as everyone had knocked everyone else onto the beds—four orange bumper cars having the time of their lives over something so simple.

Richard knew that it was entirely natural to think about earlier times when you were on the verge of ending something as major in your life as a marriage. But thinking about the past just made you feel worse. The fact was that ending a relationship was sad. It was depressing.

Even if you yourself wanted the divorce, that didn't insulate you from the loss you would feel. Richard knew from his work that it was a myth to believe that the person filing the divorce would leave the courthouse skipping and jumping with joy. That was the exception, never the rule.

The more likely scenario was that both parties would need some time to work through the loss. No one had a corner on the market of emotional pain following a divorce.

He knew the drill. He'd slowly piece his life together and so would Laura. They had no choice. Emotional survival depended on adapting, especially for the sake of Sandi and Christa.

Getting divorced would just legalize their emotional estrangement. Neither of them had been happy during the past few years. Then why did he feel so bad about it? Why were these letters making him feel so sad? They were about his parents' relationship not his own. Then it suddenly occurred to him. It had been staring him in the face for the past three hours.

Richard wished the words he had been reading weren't penned by his father. *He wanted them to be his words.*

Reaching into his briefcase, he took out his pen and a pad of paper. There was something he needed to do.

But first, he wanted to finish reading what his mother had written that year.

Dear Christopher,

I'm taking an inventory. Let's see.

Forty years of marriage. Four children, nine grand-children. The years have gone by too quickly. As we get older, I can see that more and more. I oftentimes find myself telling the girls to enjoy these years to the fullest. They will never come again.

When I watch them with their families, I see that, though times have changed, the responsibilities haven't. I seem to have forgotten how much work keeping up with a nine-year-old entails. When I watch Marcia and David, though, I'm reminded.

One of the pleasures of being at this point in life is that we can enjoy the grandchildren, then give them back. You know, Christopher, I devoted so much of my life to raising the children.

It was difficult at first when Richard finally left and I had to accept the fact that that part of my life was complete. It was a tough adjustment for me, but now I have found new pleasures in life I never had time to enjoy.

I now enjoy reading and spending time with you. I especially like our evening walks or glass of wine on the porch. We have time to talk. We had such little time and energy for that when we were raising the children.

I also believe that a key to our finding more happiness together in the past few years has been finding balance. You have your friends and I have mine. We both value our marriage but want some independence as well.

There's also the fact that we have become wiser over the years, more accepting of each other. We could have saved each other a lot of grief if we'd figured that out sooner. But I suppose wisdom can't be rushed.

You continue to be a wonderful father and husband. I try to let you know that often. I appreciate our affection for one another. I never tire of holding hands or stroking your hair, nor do I tire of your touch.

You are quite the lover . . . passionate and exciting.

Love,
Sarah

Richard closed his eyes for a moment.

He imagined sitting in the front row of a movie theater and then slowly moving backward row by row. He could see the details directly in front of him. Each individual conflict had been clear at the time, but now he was seeing something else: the *bigger picture*.

The bigger picture was about understanding how all the pieces fit together. The farther you moved back from the situation, the clearer it became. Without this viewpoint, it didn't make any overall sense. The anniversary letters revealed the importance of perspective.

But perspective was difficult to achieve without experience. It seemed to Richard that you needed to go through it firsthand to truly discover what it was all about. As his mother had written earlier, wisdom can't be rushed.

Forty-Seventh Year

R ichard knew that year forty-seven was an important anniversary in his parents' marriage. It was the last year in which they would both be unaware of what lay directly ahead of them. He guessed that the exchange would reveal more of what he had just read. They would write about how settled their lives had become and how much they were enjoying these years together.

Dear Sarah,

Happy anniversary, darling! I am so happy to see that our lives are going so well. I truly feel fortunate that we have these precious years to enjoy together.

I am so looking forward to the around-the-world trip we've planned for our fiftieth anniversary. I don't think I can wait the three years. I must study the brochures at length at least twice a week. I know how excited you are, too. I'm so glad Tom and Margaret can go with us. They are wonderful friends.

Well, in the meantime, I think we will have to practice our cruising skills and go to Alaska this summer. What do you think?

Until now, I never believed the saying "Youth is wasted on the young." I am having a ball with you. The advantage at our age is that we have fulfilled our responsibilities to the children. They all are doing so well.

I'm not so sure about Richard, though. He and Laura seem strained, though they try to keep it to themselves. I know from our talks that you sense it too. When you know your children so well, there isn't much they can hide from you.

I think your calling Laura and letting her know you're there to talk was kind. It's one of those qualities I admire about you—your ability to be there for all your family, including your sons- and daughter-in-law. I can see that Laura appreciated it, even if she does not take advantage of the offer.

Well, Sarah, after forty-seven years of marriage, we have our family, our health, our love for each other and our good friends.

I end this anniversary letter a content and grateful man.

Love,
Christopher

Richard had never known that his mother had extended an invitation to Laura to talk. It didn't surprise him, though. His mother had a big heart and enough room to include everyone in the family without passing judgment.

As he thought about it for a moment, Richard realized that it was a characteristic his parents had always shared. Neither of them was particularly judgmental. Looking back over the years, Richard knew that they certainly had their opinions on various matters, but they had never minded entertaining other points of view.

With the notable exception of political matters, Richard thought as he recalled their discussions about the Vietnam War and Communism.

Richard looked at his watch, thinking that he'd better move on with his reading.

Dear Christopher,

Happy anniversary, honey! I feel very fortunate. I'm not sure exactly why, but this year in particular has been one in which I feel truly settled.

I have enjoyed our relationship immensely. I never knew we still had this much in common until we had the opportunity to spend so much time together.

Our evening walks and conversations late into the night are something I look forward to each and every day. It's funny how we seem to talk about all kinds of matters, but the conversation eventually turns back to the children and their families. I suppose that's natural.

I enjoy our friendships as well. We never seem to have had enough time to spend nurturing our relationships with others when we were raising the family. It's good to get close to friends our own age who share a common historical and cultural background.

I am so excited about our upcoming travel plans. I so want to see Alaska, and the trip around the world will be wonderful.

We live in exciting and challenging times, Christopher. I am happy to be alive.

I look forward to the trip in three years, but in some ways it seems so far off. I want to live for the moment. I don't take any day of my life for granted and thank God for each minute on this earth. While I look forward to fulfilling some of our dreams in the future, I also know that I have achieved what I wanted. The children are all settled.

I did have a lengthy discussion with Laura recently. She's a fine woman and has a good head on her shoulders. Since her own mother died when she was so young, I sense she has kept much inside.

Laura loves Richard very much. She's just overwhelmed by all the responsibilities of raising two daughters and also having a busy career. She understands Richard's frustrations, but she feels isolated, too. Most of all, she misses his friendship.

I told her how you and I struggled through similar times. I think it helped her, but only time will tell.

I let her know that whatever happens between them will not diminish our relationship with Sandi and Christa, and that we want to remain in Laura's life as well, if that's possible.

No matter how old your children are, Christopher, they're always your children, aren't they?

Well, my love, keep planning our adventures together.

Love,
Sarah

Richard was surprised—and thankful—that his mother had talked to Laura in this way. He wondered if they had other conversations over the years that he never knew about. They probably did. Richard wished he could have been a fly on the wall during those discussions. Whatever the nature of their conversations, Richard could trust that his mother had been fair and objective.

Year Forty-Eight

Richard's mother was diagnosed with cancer in year forty-eight. The whole family was devastated by the news.

His sisters and he had pulled together as best they could and had done a good job of supporting their parents. They all took turns going to San Francisco to help their mother as she grew weaker, a result of both the advancing disease and the aftereffects of the chemotherapy.

It was difficult because the family was so spread out geographically. By this time, Marcia's husband had been transferred to London. It was especially hard for her being so many thousands of miles away. Marie still lived in Boston and Suzanne lived in Phoenix. With Richard in Miami, it was difficult for them all to connect.

Still, the years and the geographic distance didn't prevent them from supporting one another. They'd grown up in a loving family, and that would see them through these painful times. Whatever petty differences lay between them vanished with the reality of their mother's diagnosis.

Richard remembered reading the report the pathologist had faxed to his office.

Acute myelogenous leukemia. Spleen and liver enlarged with secondary metastasis.

As a doctor, he knew what that meant.

Richard had quickly scanned to the end of the report to see what was written under the heading titled "prognosis." He already knew what he would find, but he needed to read the words himself. "The patient's prognosis is poor."

Richard remembered his own desperate hope that she would be the exception to the rule. She would be the patient who survived, stumping all the doctors.

So many strides had been made in the treatment of cancer. His own sister, Marcia, had been diagnosed with lymphoma five years earlier.

That would have been during his parents' forty-third year of marriage, and the letters from that particular anniversary year were missing. It had been a scary time for the whole family, and Richard thought that maybe there were some things about that time that his father found unnecessary or too private to share.

With the help of a bone-marrow transplant from Marie, Marcia had been successfully treated. Her twin sister had turned out to be what her oncologist had called her "ace in the hole," a perfect match that other marrow recipients could only dream about.

But his mother's case had been different. Richard had known that she would be in for the struggle of her life.

Treatment would be aggressive and involve blood transfusions. Cytotoxic agents would be administered, likely bringing a temporary reprieve from the effects of the illness. But because of its advanced stage, Richard had realized immediately that it was only a matter of time.

Richard now resolved that he would read these last two letters in the spirit that his father intended when he gave them to Richard. They were letters about life, not death.

Dear Sarah,

I will be with you every second of every hour of every day.

I love you with all my heart,
Christopher

At first glance, Richard thought that the letter said too little about such an important year. He looked for a second page but found none. At second glance, he realized it said everything.

His mother's letter was much longer.

Dear Christopher,

This letter will find its way to you. I've decided to leave you all of them after I'm gone. It was never my intention

to share them with you, but this year's events have caused me
to think and reflect on many things, so I've reconsidered.

I will not lie to you. My outside veneer of confidence is
for everyone else. I don't want you and the children to
suffer any more than necessary. But I know that you can
see right through this facade and I thank you for not
challenging it. We must all use whatever tools we have at our
disposal to get us and our loved ones through as best we can.

I am afraid, but not for the reasons one might imagine.
I'm sixty-eight years old now and, you know from our
talks, well aware of my own mortality.

I am afraid for you and the children. I have cared for
my family all my life and even watched over you whenever
you were ill. I never envisioned I would be the one who
needed care. It must be the way mothers are programmed
by nature. We don't think about ourselves very often.

I don't want to be a physical or emotional burden, but
I will be. What I want is quickly becoming separate from
reality. It's as if my life is now completely out of my
control. There is nothing I can do to change that. It's a
strange feeling.

What I do have control over is my dignity.

My deepest fears are that you will come to know me as
fragile and helpless. I want to be able to care for myself.

Mortality is not something we think about in our youth.

It comes with the passage of age or learning of the death of someone we love. We have experience with both, don't we?

When we're young we think we'll live forever. Death seems like an abstraction, something that happens to others.

We haven't spoken much about religion over the years. Though I grew up as a Catholic, I haven't practiced it as well as I should have. Impending death forces you to think about such matters. Even the atheist in the most private of moments can't help but wonder.

I really don't know what will happen after I die. As you know, I've always substituted the word nature for God. How could one argue that one's life energy wasn't going back into the flow of life that is nature? What does it matter what we call it?

There's a force at work that is much more powerful than any of us, that's for certain. What form that energy takes is unknown to me.

I do know that what matters in this life is how we touch others, the care and concern we show for each other.

We have taught our children well. They all understand that there is richness to be found in their relationships and that true poverty is the absence of caring for others. Their actions prove that they've learned well.

I am most worried about Richard and Laura.

They're having such problems. I hope they find it in

themselves to work through their difficulties. They're both wonderful people who are, in my judgment, simply lost right now. Their lives have become so complicated. They have so many things to handle.

I don't want any of my children to be unhappy, and I include all their spouses as our family. Together with our children, they are the parents of our grandchildren. How could they not forever remain family?

If Richard and Laura find that divorce is the only solution for them, then so be it. I just want them to be happy, and Sandi and Christa to be all right.

Now it's your turn, Christopher.

I am so grateful that you came into my life. You are a wonderful man and I am so proud to be your wife. I hope you've been proud to be my husband. After forty-eight years of marriage, we've long ago worked out our differences, which were, upon reflection, petty and meaningless. They didn't seem so meaningless at the time, though, did they?

You are perfect for me and have been since the day we met. I don't know if there are mysterious and magical forces at work that bless certain couples, but we were blessed. Blessed even though there were times when we felt cursed.

We didn't realize at the time that we were a perfect couple. We thought the differences meant something. They were really just minor matters in an otherwise architecturally perfect relationship.

That's one of the secrets of life I've discovered: My relationships are all perfect; it's my perception of them that's been a problem at times. Conflict and disappointment are all part of the territory. Even in our moments of greatest loneliness in each other's presence, we never realized how close we were. We have always been more alike than not.

It's strange that in life these insights aren't available to us to weave into the daily fabric of our lives as they unfold. It is only upon reflection that one finds some peace. When we were in the thick of it, I doubt we would have understood or accepted these concepts.

It's hard to remain philosophical when responsibility overwhelms you. But this philosophy is exactly what got us through—a deep, unspoken and at times seemingly fragile commitment to each other and our love.

We all have limited time on this earth. I want to make each moment of each day as full of life as possible. With your love and your help, that wish will be realized.

You'll never know how much your words meant to me this year.

I love you always and forever,
Sarah

So far, the letters had stirred a debate between Richard's head and his heart. The timeless dance between the intellect and emotions had engaged him. This dance that could drive one crazy—he'd seen it a thousand times in his practice. Love could turn your guts inside out like nothing else.

All of a sudden, the debate stopped. Richard saw that it was as simple and as complicated as this: *The mind has no heart of its own, but the heart has a mind of its own.*

Sometimes the most irrational decisions end up being the smartest of all. Why not take a risk? What did he have to lose?

Now I'm really losing it, Richard thought. *A little clarity of mind would be nice right about now.*

Richard took the rest of the papers and put them on the seat next to him. He folded his hands together, took a deep breath and closed his eyes.

He focused his attention on three words.

Calm. Peaceful. Relaxed.

It was a technique he often used to reach a level of deep relaxation and to settle his thoughts. He wanted to bypass his critical mind for a moment or two. He also wanted to move beyond his emotions to that place in his mind that was at peace.

Calm. Peaceful. Relaxed.

He repeated the words over and over again in his mind. Slowly. Deliberately. He imagined himself on a beach, enjoying the peaceful rhythm of the waves meeting the shore. The sounds around him helped guide him to a deeper state of relaxation.

Calm. Peaceful. Relaxed. In a few minutes Richard was deeply and completely relaxed.

He felt something familiar yet at the same time distant stir inside him. He knew that if he resisted any temptation to analyze it, it would become stronger. The feeling grew stronger as he recognized it as something beyond his reason and his emotions. *It was his intuition and it had something important to communicate.*

Opening his eyes, Richard once again looked at his watch. The flight was due in Miami in about an hour. This moment would never come again, and he realized he couldn't afford the luxury of waiting another hour.

His intuition told him a window of opportunity was open right now.

Turbulence

R ichard picked up the air phone in front of him. He swiped his credit card through and dialed. As he waited for the call to connect, he thought to himself what paradoxical times these were.

Americans were living in the midst of a communications revolution: beepers, faxes, the Internet, email, voice mail, answering machines, cellular phones, air phones. There really wasn't any excuse for not keeping in contact.

At the same time, many people were out of touch with each other. Out of touch with what really mattered. Communications were often reduced to sound bites with little or no substance.

He'd traveled to many other cultures where people took the time to connect. A few summers ago, while he and Laura had traveled through

Europe, he had admired how the Italians sat for hours over dinner and a few bottles of wine, taking the time to know each other. The face-to-face relationship was everything.

He could hear the phone beginning to ring on the other end. He wasn't sure whether or not Laura would be home yet. She'd been working on a big case recently and she might still be at the office.

Richard had already decided that if the machine picked up, he'd just hang up. He wasn't interested in leaving any messages. He believed that if it was meant to be she would be there. For a split second, Richard thought about hanging up.

What was he doing? Did he really think Laura was going to be receptive to anything he was about to say? Hell, he didn't even know *what* he was going to say.

Were the anniversary letters just seducing him into thinking he could even hope to save his marriage? Maybe he should just hang up and get a grip. He'd feel better soon enough. Going through with the divorce was the right decision. He was just vulnerable right now.

Just as he began to pull the receiver away from his ear, Richard heard Laura's voice. The static made her seem so distant. That certainly fit the scene.

"Hello?" Her voice carried with it a hint of irritation.

After living with someone for fifteen years, you could tell a lot about someone's mood through a subtle tonal inflection. She had probably just walked though the door. Their timing was rarely in sync.

"Laura, it's me, Richard." His tone of voice was gentle. He wanted her to be receptive to what he was about to say.

"Hello, Richard." Laura's voice immediately softened. "How are you?"

"Not very good, but I need to talk to you." His voice grew even more subdued. He wanted to disarm her. Still, he sounded assured, not tentative. Richard wanted her to sense his sincerity, that what he was about to say would come from a position of conviction and strength, not weakness. "Look, Laura, I know this sounds crazy but I want to try again."

There, he had said it. He blurted it out without any window dressing. Direct and to the point. He realized that it probably wasn't the best strategy when you're trying to get your spouse to reconsider preserving your marriage. You don't just penetrate layers of defenses and years of turmoil with a statement like "Let's try again." But Richard felt an urgency to act.

Strange how seconds drag when fate hangs in the balance. Maybe they were disconnected. Maybe his words had just traveled into space with no destination and no recipient.

"Richard." Laura's voice was calm and soft.

Richard thought that maybe she was going to agree. Maybe she'd come to the same conclusion but had been afraid to ask him. "I'm very sorry about your mother. I wanted so much to call you to see how you were doing, but I felt like I needed to respect your privacy because of what's going on between us. She was such a special person. I feel very lucky that she was a part of my life and I'll miss her very much. So will the girls." Laura stopped for just a moment and Richard could hear a sigh on the other end. "But we're not trying again. I just don't have it in me anymore."

Richard could sense that she was breaking down now as she said, "I have to get off the phone now."

There wasn't any opportunity to respond. The dial tone said it all.

Richard wondered what his problem was. He must be crazy to even have called. He knew their marriage was way past the point of no return.

Their problems had reached critical mass for marital failure a long time ago. A dramatic phone call from a plane speeding home would not change anything. The marriage was over and that was that. Richard had to accept it.

"Screw these anniversary letters," he muttered aloud angrily and jammed the phone back into its cradle.

Year Forty-Nine

After what had just happened, Richard felt like the last thing he wanted to do was read another letter. But he'd come this far and there was only one set left. He couldn't blame the outcome of the phone call on the letters. He'd decided to take a risk and lost.

Richard knew that this last letter would be particularly painful. Still, it wouldn't be nearly as difficult for him to read as it had been for his father to write.

My beloved Sarah,

This is the hardest anniversary letter of all, but I will keep my promise to write from my heart, as always. I am filled with fear facing the prospect of losing you. We've been through so much together, after so many years.

I love you more than you can ever know, always have, always will. From the very first moment I saw you I was more attracted to you than anyone else in my life, and that has never changed. Do you still remember the night we met? I do.

A friend and I were going to the local fair just to have some fun. I remember that I wasn't particularly looking for girls that night. I was waiting in line for the Ferris wheel and my friend, who was afraid of heights, told me to go by myself.

I remember glancing around when you caught my eye. I saw you walking from a distance. With each step, as you drew closer, I thought you looked more and more attractive. The white sweater draped over your shoulders complemented your blue dress. I was glad you were alone.

I'm not sure how or why I found the courage, but when I asked if you wanted a partner to ride with, I was thrilled that you said yes. It was funny that your friend was also afraid of heights. Of course, it was really fate at work.

I remember thinking, "Who cares about the ride when this beautiful girl just said yes to sitting next to me." I fantasized that we would be stuck at the top for a long time, trapped by circumstances and fate so we'd have an opportunity to get to know each other better.

It turned out that I didn't need a faulty Ferris wheel to further my desires. The rest of the evening was so much fun. We must have ridden each ride ten times and I wanted the night never to end.

We walked back to your parents' house. I can still see the light on the porch shimmering over your hair, illuminating your features. You thanked me for the evening and gave me a quick kiss on the cheek. I think I floated home.

But it was the kiss we gave each other on the fourth date that was the most incredible kiss of my life. You controlled it from the start, but I let you.

Your warm lips moved gently over mine, a slow buildup to gain my undivided attention. I can feel even now the slow, steady pressure as you moved your body closer against mine. Then you placed your hands gently on the back of my head as you kissed me deeply, running your fingers teasingly through my hair.

Our bodies were pressed close together and your hands caressed my shoulders before moving over my back. I was completely lost in you. Your gentleness turned to firmness as I felt the kind of forcefulness that comes with the conviction that you have found exactly what you've been looking for. There was no uncertainty in your actions, no hesitation.

It wasn't just sexual energy. It was a sense that our souls had connected, we had bonded in that mysterious way that only men and women can connect. There is no mistaking it. If it happens once in your lifetime, you know it. Even if I'd never seen you again, there was nothing that could have changed the power and enchantment of that moment.

There is magic in the world, isn't there, Sarah?

I am afraid we will not make it to our fiftieth, but I thank God for every day that your spirit remains on this earth. You are so courageous. The chemotherapy treatments are hell for you. I know that. Seeing you suffer so deeply makes me feel very helpless inside. I want so much to be able to bear the pain for you. Knowing I can't makes me all the more frustrated.

What a tragedy to have the memories of our first kiss together contained within the same letter that includes the word "chemotherapy." Still, it does come down to this, doesn't it? A lifetime together robbed in a heartbeat. I am not bitter, Sarah, only grateful for all these years I've had with you. You made my life much more complete.

I have no complaints this year, only gratitude. You are the most wonderful mother and wife any man could desire.

I want you to know that I've learned a thing or two over the years, Sarah.

Commitment and love do endure all disappointment, suffering and hardship.

My feelings today are dominated by fear. I pray each night that I will have another day with you. I also have a confession: I don't want to be in this world without you. Our purpose is complete. The children have turned out wonderfully. We wanted a better life for them. Every parent has that wish. We did well together.

No. We did famously together.

All my love,
Christopher

It was time to read his mother's words. That was about all he could do right now. Read, but not process.

My dearest Christopher,

Writing from the heart is easy. The words flow without difficulty as my heart finds another way to express itself, to show its soul. I know that the chances of us reaching our fiftieth anniversary together are at best slim now. It's only a number. Our forty-nine years of marriage have been a blessing to me. Yes, Christopher, even the hard times.

I want you to know I am happy it's me and not you. I always feared you'd die before me and I'd be heart-broken. I do not wish to die, yet I feel I have had a full life with many riches. If one understands the bigger picture, then even the hard times are a privilege.

As I've mentioned, I fully intend for you to uncover these letters after I am gone. I hope you are not too angry with me for keeping them from you. Much of what is contained in them has been discussed openly and will be no surprise. Some of it, no doubt, will be.

I know the knowledge of my affair many years ago will hurt you. I have elected to include it only to let you feel some sense of vindication. We were both wrong in so many ways. When we searched out others it was never out of a need for love, but to satisfy other needs.

There are some things that I need you to know. They are my final wishes and go beyond material concerns, as those are well covered in my will.

When I think about you being alone in this world, it causes me sadness. And I want you to know that when I am gone, you should do your best to live life to its fullest. We have a large family that needs its father and grandfather. I hope you find it within yourself to seek out others who love and support you.

Everyone knows you to be a private man, Christopher, a man who keeps much to himself. Only I know the inner you. Try to reach out to others for your own support. The children especially want to be there for you. I know this because I've spoken to each one about it. Promise me you won't shut everyone out.

There's something else, Christopher. It's a delicate matter but one that I feel strongly about.

If you feel the need and have the opportunity to find comfort and companionship with someone else, I condone it. Trust that I know that there is no one who can diminish what we have had for each other. I have also talked to the children about this and they understand.

I want you to know how very much I love you, Christopher.

And yes, if I had to do it all over again it would be with you.

I love you now and for always,
Sarah

Arrival

The wheels touched down at Miami International Airport and the aircraft briefly bounced back up into the air before settling onto the runway. For an instant, Richard hoped that the plane would just climb back up into the clouds. It would then fly far away from this world below that could cause so much pain.

He held all the anniversary letters tightly in his hands and wondered what it was all about.

Why couldn't he and Laura have shown each other the same commitment his parents had? His parents had made it through times that made their own problems seem minor by comparison. It was almost embarrassing.

By this time, he clearly understood that the answer wasn't a question of rocket science. It was obvious. They had failed to stay focused on what was really important.

He and Laura simply didn't take care of each other enough.

As the aircraft taxied to the gate, Richard resolved that he would never read the anniversary letters again. They just made him feel more like a failure. His father hadn't meant them to, of course. It was just the net result.

He gathered his belongings and made his way to the front of the cabin. He watched the older couple he'd spoken to earlier walk off, knowing he would never see them again. How he wished he and Laura could be together for that many years to come. But it was too late for that. Richard exited the plane and moved through the jetway. He walked briskly through the crowd of people who had gathered at the gate to meet their loved ones. He wasn't interested in seeing any displays of affection. He'd had enough emotional stimulation for one night.

"Richard!" The voice was unmistakable.

He turned around to see Laura standing a few feet away.

"Can I talk to you for a minute?" Her tone of voice was soft. He walked up to her and instinctively embraced her.

That emotional impulse came a fraction of a second before the intellectual shock of seeing her there. He was happy to see her and he wasn't able or willing to analyze anything at the moment.

"Sure. Is everything all right? The girls okay?" His response could hardly hide his excitement.

"Yes. They're fine. I just want a few minutes of your time. Can we go somewhere and talk?" Laura asked the question in a way that suggested she would have left politely if he declined the offer.

"Yes. Sure. Okay. Of course." He stumbled over his own affirmations. They turned to walk but Richard stopped in his tracks. He couldn't wait the couple of minutes it would take to get to the lounge.

As he gently but firmly placed his hand on her shoulder to turn her toward him, he asked, "What's going on?"

"We'll talk in just a minute, Richard. Let's go." For the next minute or so, he'd have to settle for that. He tried to read her body language for clues.

Her blond hair was still damp. She must have just jumped in the shower and hadn't had time to dry her hair completely. She wore a black knee-length dress with silver studs on the shoulders. It was one of his favorites. *That's a good sign,* he thought. Laura had selected a dress she knew he liked.

His excitement soon tempered when he realized that she was carrying a brown envelope under her arm. He glanced down and saw the name in the corner: Schiller, Stevens and Armstrong.

Richard's heart sank.

That was the name of the law firm Laura was using to represent her in the divorce. *Great,* he thought. *She's going to try to negotiate a deal right here when I'm at an all-time low.* He felt himself getting angry and his muscles tightened automatically—a response that signaled he and Laura were about to do battle. It was a familiar feeling and one that he had hoped to never experience again.

They walked through the long concourse toward the main terminal. With each step, Richard's sense of anticipation heightened. He looked ahead and saw the cultural diversity of the travelers passing through Miami International Airport. He searched for a quick mental diversion and thought about something he had considered many times before.

Each person came from somewhere and each had a story of his or her own.

How strange, he thought. No one would guess that he was walking through the airport with his soon-to-be ex-wife, having just returned from his mother's funeral. He and Laura were just another couple walking through an airline terminal. *Could anyone match our story?* he wondered for a moment.

Richard concluded in an instant, *Probably, and then some.* But this was about his and Laura's story right now, not anyone else's.

They found a quiet corner in a nearby lounge and ordered drinks. He looked at her face and hair and thought about how much he would love to slowly stroke them. After all these years he was still very attracted to her. He quickly dismissed the thought as he looked down at the envelope that she now placed on the table between them.

"What's this all about, Laura?" His tone had changed to one that was clearly guarded.

"Richard, I want you to know something. I know that calling me wasn't an easy thing to do." Laura paused for a moment. Whatever was coming next wasn't easy for her.

"I'm sorry I was so abrupt, but it's very hard for me. You know me, Richard. I plan everything. I need to control all that I can. But when you called me an hour ago, there was something I couldn't control. I hadn't planned on how I felt after I got off the phone."

She was beginning to let down her guard now. Her voice was changing to that softer, more gentle pitch he knew so well but had missed for so long.

"I love you and I do want to try again."

It was so like Laura. She got right to the point. But coming here to the airport was so unlike her.

She wasn't the kind of woman who easily gave up her defenses.

Richard felt shocked. He looked into her eyes and found the sincerity and conviction that she always had when she spoke from the heart. If he admired one thing about her, it was her conviction and passion. She was clear on the issues for which she stood. Richard knew that her presence at this moment meant something very important. She clearly wanted to be there.

The tears were rolling slowly down Laura's cheeks. This wasn't easy for her. She was letting her guard down and opening her heart. She was beginning to sob now.

Whatever defenses remained, they all surrendered to a deeper truth: the truth that she was still in love with Richard even after all the pain they had inflicted on each other. He needed to see that for himself. It was something that could never be conveyed over an air phone.

Richard moved over next to her and gently wiped the tears from her eyes. He held her tightly and closed his eyes. Maybe he hadn't been so crazy to follow his intuition after all. He wouldn't be holding her now, hearing these words, if he hadn't made the call.

"Laura, I have something for you to read."

He reached into his jacket pocket and pulled out a letter.

"I wrote this just before I called you from the plane. It's a little crumpled because I planned to throw it away after you said you wouldn't try again."

Laura unfolded the letter carefully, unsure of what it contained.

Dear Laura,

Everything is in place for the divorce—everything, that is, except for my heart.

I realize that this letter is all about taking a risk. I'm expecting you'll probably blow it off but I'm writing this so you'll read it without any immediate pressure to respond. I have one request. Just read it carefully and think it over.

Something has happened to me over the past several days since my mother died. It hit me harder than I thought it would, especially because of what you and I are going through. But this letter is not about me, it's about you.

I was about to board the plane to come home when my father handed me a package. It contained letters written between my father and mother over the course of their marriage. All you need to know is that these letters were rich and powerful.

Reading them has made me appreciate you much more deeply.

I want you to know a secret that I've kept from you for far too long. It's a secret that has lain beneath all the debris that collected as our marriage crumbled.

I love you, with all my heart.

You may find that hard to understand considering how much we seem to resent each other at times, but it's clear to me now how it's possible: I've failed to appreciate you enough, Laura.

I know our marriage has many problems. Saying these things won't make everything all right. We have a long way to go and maybe we'll never get there, but know this: I want to keep trying.

I've also discovered something else. We don't have to ever get to the point of having a perfect marriage to be happy.

I want to share a short story that helps explain how I feel.

In my practice I recently was treating a woman with marital problems. I asked her what she thought the bottom-line problem was and she stated without hesitation, "My husband's a pessimist and I'm an optimist. He sees the glass as half empty and I see it as half full."

Laura, I told this woman to go home and tell her husband that the optimists are always right. "Why is that?" she asked.

"Because your husband doesn't get the point. Life doesn't hold any promise that there should be anything in the glass. We're responsible for filling it any way we can. And tell him to be grateful for half of something!"

I realize that I need to do a better job of living these words. I need to be an optimist. Life is too short to be anything else.

I also realized something even more important while reading the anniversary letters. Over time, my parents took the optimist/pessimist glass and cut it in half. After that, it was always full. Their expectations changed with the realities of life and they matured as a couple.

It will be a struggle at times. That's our chemistry, isn't it? I'm realistic about that, but something is different now.

I feel hope.

*Our marriage can improve and we can be happier. It will get better.
I know that if I learn to understand you better, and accept you for who
you are instead of feeling frustrated because you're not what I expect,
we'll both do better.*

I need to cut the glass in half.

I know now that that doesn't mean settling. Rather, it means accepting.

*We need to give each other another chance. We've had many good
times together and there can be many more.*

Remember that whatever you decide, I will always love you.

Richard

Laura was uncharacteristically quick in her response.

"Sometimes our chemistry is just right." Laura smiled. "We're
in sync on this one, Richard. And there's something else."

Richard wondered what was coming.

"When you called me from the plane I was on my way out
the door. You won't believe where I was heading."

She was laughing nervously now the way she did when she
was releasing tension.

"I had the divorce papers in hand and was about to head
over to the attorney's office to drop them off."

"Window of opportunity," Richard responded with a smile.

"What are you talking about?" Laura looked puzzled.

"I'll tell you about it later."

"Okay, Richard, but in the meantime, I hope you don't mind if I do this."

Before he had a chance to respond, Laura took the envelope she'd been carrying and neatly ripped it in half.

"Here, Richard, help me." She handed him the two halves.

"I'd be happy to." With that confirmation, Richard tore the half into quarters, rose from his chair and threw the papers in a nearby garbage can.

He returned to the table and could see her wheels turning. But it wasn't her usual look of intellectual concentration. It was as if she knew something intuitively. Something beyond reason and analytical thinking.

But how could she? Laura wasn't the intuitive type, and besides, she didn't know what was in the anniversary letters.

He couldn't help but ask, "So, what do you think about all this?"

Laura answered with an assurance that left no doubt about its origin. "I think your parents are very wise people, Richard."

Richard pulled Laura close to him and held her tightly. For the first time in many months, his defenses fell under the power and magic of the love he felt for her.

He hoped that they would share many more anniversaries together. From the look in Laura's eyes, he sensed that she just might feel the same way.

About the Author

ichael A. Adamse received his Ph.D. in clinical psychology from the University of Miami and completed a predoctoral fellowship at Yale University. He currently holds an appointment as adjunct assistant professor of psychology at the University of Miami, and lectures worldwide for Nova Southeastern University.

Dr. Adamse specializes in relationship issues and has been in practice for over twenty years. In 1986 he started his private practice in Boca Raton, Florida. Dr. Adamse and his colleague Dr. Sheree Motta have coauthored and coproduced the audiocassette *Coupling.*

Their recently published book, *Online Friendship, Chatroom Romance and Cybersex* (Health Communications, 1996), represents a cutting-edge study of relationships online. He has appeared on MS-NBC, *The Sally Jesse Raphael Show, Maureen O'Boyle* and *20/20*, and has been the subject of numerous radio and newspaper interviews.

Dr. Adamse is currently at work on his second novel.

Born near Stockholm, Sweden, Dr. Adamse has been married for fourteen years to Diane Leeds, a prominent attorney in Palm Beach. They have two children, Elise, who is twelve, and Dana, who is nine.

Comments are welcome:

Dr. Michael Adamse
1515 North Federal Highway, #404
Boca Raton, Florida 33432
email: dradamse@gate.net

Ordinary People
Extraordinary Lives

Healing an Angry Heart

Bill Chickering & Cardwell C. Nuckols, Ph.D.

This compelling book takes a candid look at anger as it is expressed in the stories of ordinary people. This collection of stories reveals special people living in this angry world who still manage to live without a jaded vision and still believe that kindness and respect matter. It is filled with stories about the fullness of life and the journeys heart and soul take on the road to recovery. Code 5173, $10.95

Emotional and Physical Separation

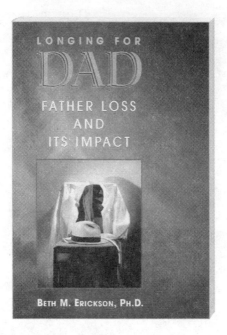

Longing for Dad
Father Loss and Its Impact
Beth M. Erickson, Ph.D.

Far from being disposable, as some contemporary voices would have us believe, fathers play a crucial role in the lives of their children. In this groundbreaking book, Dr. Beth Erickson helps readers and therapists identify and pinpoint the causes of father hunger, and explore the spiritual crises that unresolved losses such as this generate. Provocative exercises present strategies for resolving these losses and escaping the cycle of anguish. This book is a roadmap that will help new fathers provide their children with a strong foundation for a healthy, well-balanced adulthood.

Code 5491, trade paper, $11.95